EP Sport Series

ep EP PUBLISHING LIMITED
1977

ep sport

hockey
for men and women

Terry Podestà

Acknowledgements

My sincere thanks are due to a number of people, particularly, amongst the ladies, to Miss J. S. Whitehead, Editor of the official magazine of the AEWHA, 'Hockey Field', for her understanding and co-operation in making available almost all the photographs of women players. In other matters I have had the generous assistance of my former opposite number on the AEWHA Coaching Sub-Committee, and now the Association's distinguished President, Mrs. Mary Russell Vick, and of their National Coach, Miss E. Stuart Smith. The lower photograph on p. 9 was kindly provided by the courtesy of the Wembley Stadium authorities. My own HA colleagues have been equally helpful with advice and with putting their own material at my disposal: Mr. C. M. Cox, a former England Juniors' Manager and my successor as Chairman of the Coaching Sub-committee, and our two National Coaches, Messrs. J. F. Cadman and T. H. E. Clarke.

Mr. D. F. Vinson, an HA Staff Coach, went to great pains specially to photograph the men's skills, in which he was patiently helped by four of his young players from the East Division: Mark Dauban, James Duthie, Leslie Johnson and Matthew Swayne. He also provided the photographs of the 1976 Olympics in Montreal.

Without the very willing help of all these, and of several others, the book would not have been written.

T.A.P.
May 1977

Cover photograph by Gerry Cranham.

Photographs on pp. 2 and 118 by Tony Duffy.

ISBN 0 7158 0578 9

Published by EP Publishing Ltd, East Ardsley, Wakefield, West Yorkshire, 1977

Text set in 10/11 pt Monophoto Univers, printed by photo-lithography and bound in Great Britain by Butler & Tanner Ltd, Frome and London

Foreword

The introduction to hockey of systems and the alteration in the offside rule has, in the last decade, brought change to the game. Terry Podestà, in 'EP Sport Hockey for Men and Women', by first setting out the techniques which need to be mastered, emphasises that technique and skill are essential for any system to succeed. In tracing the history of systems he points out that whichever one is chosen, it should increase the efficiency of the team to the greatest possible extent, having due regard to the strengths and weaknesses of the players. His broad-minded approach to the game makes this book of interest to women as well as men and readers are encouraged to adopt and adapt according to their ability and the circumstances rather than conform to one particular set pattern.

At a time when tactics are being constantly rethought, players and coaches will welcome this book written by a person who, as Chairman of the Coaching Committee of the Hockey Association for many years, has been in close touch with the latest developments. How fortunate that, on his retirement from that office, he has found time to put his ideas on paper for the benefit of all hockey players.

MARY RUSSELL VICK

Contents

England Club Champions, 1976
The Nottingham Hockey Club European Cup Squad
Standing (*left to right*):
N. Cassell, C. Walters, M. Boddington, B. Gill, J. Sharpe, W. R. Sissons, J. Starling,
C. R. Scott (Manager)
Kneeling (*left to right*):
M. Harvey, H. R. A. Stokes, M. Watson (Vice-Captain), M. Elson (Captain), J. M. Appleby,
M. Alderson, J. R. Maughan
Also in squad: C. Anderson and J. Stanyard

England—
IFWHA Champions
Edinburgh, 1975

Three exceptional English post-war forwards. From left to right, Vera Chapman, Mary Russell Vick (now President of the AEWHA and here scoring in a 9–2 rout of Scotland at Wembley) and Jo Hamilton-Bates

Preface

The Hockey Association was founded in 1886. Nine years later they declined a request for affiliation to them by the ladies. They had, they said, 'been formed entirely in the interests of men's clubs'. The ladies therefore founded the All-England Women's Hockey Association, though they adopted the men's rules.

Each association amended the rules to suit themselves so that in time differences became marked. The ladies' first change was to decree that 'No player shall wear a hat-pin'!

About thirty years after the formation of the AEWHA, the four Home Countries and another four set up the International Federation of Women's Hockey Associations. One of the aims was to work for uniformity of rules.

Around this time the men's international body, the Fédération Internationale de Hockey, was also formed. Amongst its members were national associations containing women's sections and these were not allowed to join IFWHA until after the war. Thus it came about that there are two international women's bodies with not all countries belonging to both FIH and IFWHA.

Whereas IFWHA laid down the rules for its affiliates, the men's rules were made by the International Hockey Board, later renamed the International Hockey Rules Board. Originally this body was totally independent but it is now a part, though an autonomous part, of the FIH. In the late 'sixties the ladies formed the Women's International Hockey Rules Board, and they and the IHRB began moving towards a common code.

Pressure had been mounting for the inclusion of Women's Hockey in the Olympics. The IOC will recognise only one international governing body for each sport. In late 1975 the IFWHA and FIH therefore set up a Supreme Council on which each Federation was equally represented, so paving the way for women to enter the 1980 Moscow Olympics.

Preceding it by a few months came the first combined code of rules, issued jointly by the IHRB and WIHRB. In only a few instances did they find it necessary to legislate separately for men and women. It is interesting to note, incidentally, that in the past the women have sometimes introduced changes in the rules subsequently copied by the men. The most notable example is probably the once so-called 'Ladies' Corner Rule'.

In the 1976 edition of 'Rules of the Game of Hockey', the only differences appear in Rule 14, Free Hit, and a related 'Guidance' note on Rule 17, I, 'Hit from 16 yards'. The Rules are referred to frequently throughout this book. Space does not allow lengthy quotations from them and for full details readers should consult an up-to-date copy of the Rules Book.

For a long time now, after the far-off days of 1895, relationships between the AEWHA and HA have been cordial. A few years ago, and at the instigation of the ladies, the Coaching Sub-Committees of the two Associations formulated a joint coaching award, the Junior Secondary Teachers' Coaching Certificate. More recently, senior officials of both Associations decided to meet regularly to discuss matters of common interest.

It is against this backcloth that I have written this book in the hope that it may help both women and men club players. Obviously there must be certain variations in the play of the two sexes, if only because of the differences in their anatomy. For convenience I have generally followed the example of the Rules Book and used the masculine gender, except in those parts of the book not relating to men. Because my own knowledge of the game is necessarily male-orientated, I hope lady readers will forgive me if inadvertently I have made any statements they consider heretical.

Note on Metrication
At the time of writing, the English Rules Book still uses Imperial measurements, and I have therefore done the same. However, the metric equivalents are given here.

Metric Equivalents

Imperial	Metric
100 yd	91.40 m
60 ,,	55.00 ,,
25 ,,	22.90 ,,
16 ,,	14.63 ,,
10 ,,	9.14 ,,
7 ,,	6.40 ,,
5 ,,	4.55 ,,
4 ,,	3.66 ,,
2 ,,	1.83 ,,
1 ,,	0.91 ,,
7 ft	2.14 ,,
5 ,,	1.50 ,,
4 ,,	1.20 ,,
18 in	46.00 cm
12 ,,	30.00 ,,
$9\frac{1}{4}$,,	23.50 ,,
$8\frac{13}{16}$,,	22.40 ,,
6 ,,	15.00 ,,
3 ,,	7.50 ,,
2 ,,	5.10 ,,
28 oz	794 g
23 ,,	652 ,,
12 ,,	340 ,,
$5\frac{3}{4}$,,	163 ,,
$5\frac{1}{2}$,,	156 ,,

As printed in the official Rules Book

Areas of the Pitch

As these will be referred to throughout the book, the meaning of the various terms should be understood.
Longitudinally the pitch is divided approximately into thirds, as shown on p. 12.
Some authorities may take the twenty-five yard lines as the relevant boundaries. In my view this is too confining, especially bearing in mind, particularly in men's hockey, the possibility of penalty corners for deliberate offences within the twenty-five yards area. Although the Rules require them to be, umpires are not clairvoyants! There is always the risk of unintentionally clumsy play being regarded as a deliberate infringement.
It is therefore safer to extend the Attack and Defence Areas beyond the twenty-fives.
For a plan of the pitch and a diagram showing the areas of the pitch, see p. 12.

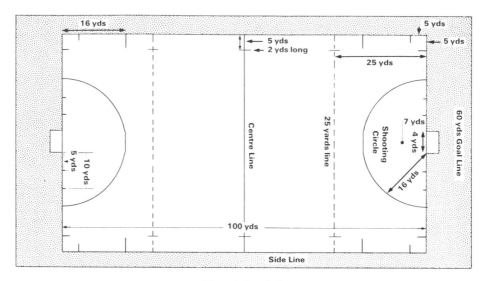

16 yds

5 yds

5 yds

5 yds
2 yds long

25 yds

Centre Line

25 yards line

Shooting Circle

7 yds

4 yds

16 yds

60 yds Goal Line

10 yds

5 yds

100 yds

Side Line

Plan of the pitch

Areas for team playing →

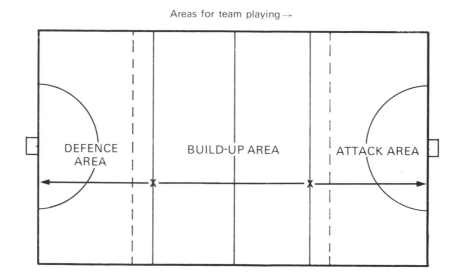

DEFENCE AREA

BUILD-UP AREA

ATTACK AREA

Equipment

Sticks (see Rule 8)

The stick needs to feel comfortable and to be readily manipulated. Individual preferences will depend on the player's height and strength. It is particularly important that youngsters' sticks are appropriate to any given stage of development. Smaller sticks are made specially. Adult sticks are usually approximately 33–36 in. Weight may be up to 23 oz for women and 28 oz for men, but the balance and feel will be influenced by the weight distribution. Those in the 16–22 oz range are mostly used. Defenders, other than goalkeepers, may prefer heavier sticks than midfields and forwards. Longer and heavier sticks are made but are less easily bought.

To assess the balance, pick up and swing the stick as if hitting the ball. It should come up without feeling clumsy. Try using the left hand only. Also, move the stick head over an imaginary ball as if dribbling.

Views will vary on the amount of 'give' desirable. Too much whippiness will reduce strength in a tussle for the ball. Whippiness does increase with use. Too stiff a stick will feel uncomfortable and hinder proper collection of a hard-hit ball.

Other points worth checking are that the handle is not too big for the hand, that there is breadth at the splice — the area where blade meets handle — and that the grain is close and even, reducing the chance of splintering. If binding ever needs to be applied, this must still allow the stick to pass through a ring 2 in. in diameter. It should be noted that splinters, sharp edges and metal insets are not allowed. The handle may be covered by a rubber grip, a towelling grip or a spiral of both. Again, the choice is a personal matter.

Sticks should be wiped clean after every match or practice and treated with an occasional application of linseed oil.

Footwear (see Rule 9(a))

Nothing dangerous is allowed, which in certain cases might rule out worn studs.

There is a number of types of suitable boots and shoes available. Some players favour boots with screw-in studs which may be varied in accordance with the pitch surface. Others prefer footwear with moulded soles and rubber studs.

The Rule Book, under 'Personal Equipment', recommends moulded rubber studs or bars.

Nowadays a great deal of hockey is played on hard surfaces. Some sort of training shoe is required for them. Studs are banned because of the damage they cause. Such shoes would also serve for indoor hockey — rapidly gaining an enthusiastic and ever-growing following — and for indoor training. A cheap pair may well prove false economy.

Footwear should always be cleaned after use.

Shinguards

Years ago many thought it effeminate for out-players to wear shinguards. Their value is now fortunately generally recognised, and so too is the value of those with extensions giving some ankle protection. Light plastic ones, backed with foam rubber, are readily obtainable.

Mouth Guards ('gum shields')

Nowadays more men wear them — and advisedly, since oral and dental injuries are fairly common. Prevention is here much better than cure, especially if this necessitates the extraction of teeth. It is far preferable for the guard to be made and fitted by the player's dentist, rather than bought in a sports shop.

Balls (see Rule 7)

Every player should have his own plastic practice ball — and use it, even in odd moments, as much as possible.

Techniques and Skills

Introductory Notes

1. Terminology

Nowadays for practical purposes it may be taken that a particular action, e.g. a push, is a technique; transferred into a game-like situation, using that term very broadly, it is influenced by outside factors, such as the proximity of opponents, and becomes a skill. Coaching aims at inculcating correct points of a given technique and then at what may be called 'grooving' the technique. The result is that the player performs the action concerned without having consciously to wonder whether, for instance, his hands are correctly placed on the stick.

2. The Coaching Grid

Parts of this chapter contain references to the grid. It is described in detail on pp. 62–3. Briefly, it is merely a useful aid to practical coaching, consisting of a number of adjoining squares marked out on the ground.

Examples of suitable exercises, in addition to those given elsewhere, appear on pp. 64–6. These should be consulted for additional practices for most sections.

3. Fitness

Fitness methods are outside the scope of this book. Fitness may be regarded as having two components, general — e.g. a sound cardio-vascular system — and specific to the game concerned. It has been defined as the ability to withstand the onset of fatigue. Obviously the unfit player cannot make his full contribution to the team effort. Skill is an early victim of fatigue. For an analysis of fitness and list of exercises, see *Conditioning for Sport* by Dr. N. Whitehead (EP Publishing Ltd., 1975).

The Push

This technique is described first for several reasons. It is the simplest of strokes and readily taught. With it, beginners find that they soon have at their command a method of propelling the ball, whereas difficulties may arise over the hit, reducing enjoyment. Further, the position of the hands is such that most other methods of controlling and moving the ball — e.g. collecting, reverse-stick techniques and the dribble — merely involve a rapid adjustment of the grip. Whilst lacking the power and distance of the hit, the push is very quick; it can be made with little warning to the opponent; and it is valuable for the rapid clearance or shot. Weighting passes is easier than with the hit and the push can also be played from difficult positions where a hit would be impossible. The push has a very wide passing arc, from about seven to four o'clock, and can be made when the player is moving fast.

For the standard technique the following apply:

- **Grip.** Left hand at the top of the stick, right lower down gripping powerfully near the middle.
- **Stance.** Side-on, left shoulder pointing at the target. The feet are well spaced, providing a strong platform. For upfield passing the left toes point much more closely towards the target than in the hit.
- **Ball.** Its position is variable, depending in part on the intended direction. For upfield it may range from much nearer the right than left foot to in advance of the left foot. For passing to the eight or seven o'clock area it will be in advance of and to the left of the left foot, whereas to play to four o'clock it will be about opposite the right foot. Players must learn to pass and shoot off the wrong foot, i.e. with the right foot forward.
- **Body.** Inclined forward with knees bent and head and eyes as nearly over the ball as possible.
- **The Stroke.** Usually said to begin with stick in contact with the ball. In practice some slight forward run of the blade along the ground up to the ball often occurs, but see The Push-In, p. 120. There is, however, no backswing.
As the stick drives forward it remains in contact with ground

Grip for both push and flick

and ball for as long as possible. It must not edge under the ball so as to cause it to lift, since, in certain circumstances – e.g. at a push-in – that would break the rules.

The left hand pulls against the thrust of the right. The wrists are firm throughout.

- **Power.** Power derives from co-ordination of the movements of the various parts of the body. The main components are the thrust of the right leg, weight transference and the strength of the right forearm and both wrists. For its full development power depends on the firm base; see 'Stance' above. The weight begins over the right foot unless the player is running. With the thrust of the

a

b

c

d

The push—side view

right leg the weight transfers to over the left foot, the right shoulder coming round towards the line of pass. The opposed action of the two hands adds to the power.

Power at a push-in is often essential.

- **Follow-through.** As in nearly all strokes, the follow-through is important, giving accuracy of direction. A good follow-through will also help to prevent the ball from rising.

Variations

Passing on the run must be perfected with a wide arc of delivery and with the player able to continue forward virtually without checking. In passing behind square, the body must twist strongly and, especially to the right, the player has to depend for power on his shoulders, arms and wrists.

With experience the push can be adapted to emergencies—e.g. straight ahead from a square-on position—though power will be reduced.

WARNING: Because of its very simplicity, almost any match will provide examples of the carelessly and sloppily played push. Coaches should instil the habit of pushing firmly and accurately.

Practices

1. To start: With the correct grip, walk up to the ball, place the stick against it, lean forward and shove! Then vary approach and direction.

2. In pairs: There are many possibilities.
— Pushing against a wall and

The push — front view

Moving into the push

returning. Improvise any necessary little rules. Start non-competitively.
— Along a line, or through a narrow 'gate', for accuracy.
— Receiver indicates with stick where partner is to push.
— Dribble forward and push to partner. Blade close to ball throughout.
— Partners stand 10 yds apart, and compete against other pairs. How many pushes in a given time, say 1 minute?

3. 3 (or 2) v. 1 play possession hockey ('keep ball') in a grid square using the push.

4. In circles: Push ball round a suitable number of players, first clockwise then anti-clockwise. Introduce second ball. Try to catch it up with first.

5. Relay Races: Team of 6 or 8 splits into two equal sections, 15–20 yds apart. First man in one section pushes to opposite number in team. He runs after his ball to join end of other section. Receiver repeats. Teams compete against each other.

6. On the Run: In pairs: First man pushes ball a few yards, pursues it, gets side-on and pushes to partner. Vary by pushing right or left. Also practise off right foot.

Dribbling

Dribbling is moving with the ball under control. Control will be lost unless blade and ball are kept closely together. Historically there are two types of dribble, the English, derived from the old long-bladed English stick which propelled the ball from behind, and the Indian. This is performed by turning the now universally accepted smaller-headed stick over the ball.

Forehand Dribble

For close contact work the English method in men's hockey began to die thirty years ago with the return of Servicemen from the Far East. This forehand dribble is, however, still used for moving with the ball to the player's right front. Hence it has the important advantage of allowing beginners to progress comparatively easily with the ball, thus heightening their enjoyment. The essentials are:
● **Grip.** Left hand at the top of the stick so that the forearm acts as a more or less straight extension of the handle. The right hand holds comfortably down the handle, increasing control without too crouched a position.
● **Ball.** Should be to the right

front, not close enough to hamper movement *or restrict vision* and not so far away as to reduce control. The stick will be at about 45° to the ground.
● **Feet and Body.** For forward progression, conditioned by the above.
● **Propulsion.** Is by a series of little taps imparted principally by the right hand.

Dribbling with the ball in this position enables greater speed over the ground when needed than the Indian method (see p. 19).

Practices

1. Dribble along a line. Dribble in various directions, as 'Follow my Leader'.

2. Divide into groups of 3. B dribbles to C and gives him the ball. C then takes it to A and so on. This can be developed as a relay, providing that players are carefully watched to ensure that the ball does not run more than, say, 1 yd ahead of the blade at first.

3. **Dribbling with a Turn.** Players line up across the pitch, each with a skittle about 15 yds in front of him. They dribble round it.
Right Turn. This needs a strong lead from the left side with left arm leading and right shoulder trailing and quick, small steps to overtake the ball. The strong left shoulder position later helps with

Above and below: The forehand dribble

passing to the right and sometimes with receiving from the right.

Left Turn. Just before reaching the skittle, bring the ball across in front of the body. Having rounded the skittle, the ball is then controlled on the right front.

4. Turn Relay — a) Developed from 2 and 3. — b) Extra skittles added to make a slalom.

The Indian Dribble

This introduces reverse-stick play. Broadly speaking, the stick is said to be reversed when the toe is pointing towards the player's body.

In the Indian dribble the ball is tapped forward diagonally in front of and across the body by the stick, alternately in the forehand and reversed positions. The blade is rotated by the left hand over and very close to the ball.

● **Grip.** It is virtually impossible to carry out the stick movements with the left hand in the English (forehand) dribble position. From this position it is gradually adjusted until the movements can be made comfortably. Placing the left thumb down the stick helps, and *players who do not do this should try it.*

Grip for Indian dribble and controlling

The right hand holds lightly about 9 in below the left. As the technique is developed, players will find that in fact both hands move to some extent.

- **Ball.** As in the forehand dribble, above, except that it is in front of the body and moves laterally about the width of the shoulders. With proficiency, much wider movements, to unsettle opponents, are possible.
- **Feet and Body.** As close to being as for normal running as the above allow.

Learning the Indian Dribble

With the hands as described above, stand facing square to the front, toes level and feet about shoulder-width apart. The arms should be bent and clear of the comfortably bent body. The ball should be at a reasonable distance in front of the right foot, with the blade on the right side of the ball. Now tap it across to a position in front of your left foot.

Simultaneously, turn the stick swiftly so that the reversed toe arrives just before it. The ball is returned to its starting position on the forehand, again with the stick just beating it.

The next stage is to move the ball continuously, without pause, from side to side. A time-based competitive element in very short spells may be helpful.

Then move with the ball at a walk. As an elementary guide, you should tap the ball from left to right as the left foot comes to the ground, and from right to left as the right foot comes to the ground. Eventually, progress to a trot and then a run, ultimately increasing this to top speed. You must also be able to move the ball backwards and forwards. This can be practised in the same sequence up to top speed.

Practices

Adapt those given for the forehand dribble.

Tactical Considerations

First, *never regard dribbling as an end in itself.* It is a comparatively slow way of moving the ball about the field. Part of the skill of dribbling is to know when *not* to use it!

Its uses are:
- To escape with the ball under control from an opponent. It is therefore a necessity for every out-player.
- To beat or draw an opponent. See p. 33.
- When awaiting support. Moving across field or in the direction where support is expected to materialise may be beneficial.
- While opening or assessing passing angles.
- To avoid passing to an offside team-mate.

Second, to achieve any of the above, you must be *aware* of your environment. This is impossible if you have to

Indian dribble

concentrate so hard on technique that you can think of nothing else, or if your eyes are glued to the ball.

Therefore players must achieve a very high level of technique and be trained to look up to scan the field. *Head up* dribbling is an essential.

Head-up dribbling

Third, it should be noted that when you are on your own and need to cover ground with the ball at the fastest rate, do *not* keep the ball near your stick. Instead play a series of short through passes to yourself until you need to regain close control.

Fourth, coaches should not generally discourage youngsters from dribbling when it is the prelude to attacking an opponent. Many players lack the ability to beat the last defender before the goalkeeper. By all means point out a gross lack of tactical appreciation, but only discourage the player actively if he becomes a show-off or a handicap to the team.

Practices

1. The coach stands in front of the players, some distance away. Players are in line abreast, adequately spaced. They dribble towards the coach, changing direction right or left in accordance

with his signals, increased in frequency as the players improve. The coach can also signal for change of speed.

2. Players, each with a ball, dribble in a confined space; depending on the numbers, say 2–4 grid squares, beginning with 2 players and feeding in others singly or in pairs. Players must not touch each other or anyone else's ball. The dribbling should not be aimless but should include changes of direction, stops and changes of pace.

3. 2 small groups of players stand about 20 yds apart. C and D set off dribbling past each other, changing course to do so, then B and E,

and so on. This can be made continuous so that, in the first instance, E does not wait for C to reach him, but sets off when C and D have crossed. So does B.

4. The players stand in 2 small areas a little distance apart, utilising say 4 grid squares. All players have a ball and begin dribbling in their own squares. On a signal Xs and Os change squares, not touching any other player or ball en route, and resume dribbling in the new square.

The Hit or Drive

This stroke, called the hit by men and the drive by women, is the most powerful of all. Its advantages lie in the speed at which the ball can be moved and the distance over which it can be made to travel. *The coach should insist on accuracy from the beginning.*

Standard method:

● **Grip.** Pick up the stick as if it were a chopper. The two Vs formed by the thumb and index finger of each hand are in line, hands hard together, left above right. Only a very small amount of stick protrudes above the left hand.

Grip for the hit or drive

● **Stance.** Stand side on, left shoulder pointing at the target and body firmly balanced. Feet should be about shoulder-width apart. Whilst the right toes will be pointing almost at right-angles to the shoulders the left toes will be at something like 30°–40°.

● **Ball** should be about in line with the left toes and at a comfortable distance from them. It must not be so far away in any direction that you have to reach out, nor so close that you lack space for a free arm action. Experiment to find your own most suitable position.

● **The Swing.** For a straight hit the backlift, downswing and follow-through should be on the same line. The so-called 'Sticks' Rule (12, l(c)) requires that no part of the stick shall be raised above

the shoulder in playing the ball. Some players infringe by cocking their wrists on the backlift, others by attempting mistakenly to obtain extra power. A fairly straight left arm, with no marked bend of the elbow, will help to avoid a breach. So will tensing the wrists at the end of the lift. This also initiates the whipping action required for power.

At contact the blade should be vertical to the ground. It strikes the ball on the 'meat' and hits through, not at, it. This will not be possible if the ball is wrongly placed.

After contact the swing continues as a smooth follow-through along the intended line of delivery. To avoid 'sticks' here the follow-through has to be checked. This is the task of the right arm which may be assisted by a slight right-to-left rolling of the wrists. Again, avoid useless cocking of the wrists. Throughout the swing the arms must move free of the body and there must be no mowing or scything action after contact.

● **Body.** On the backswing the weight is evenly distributed but begins to transfer towards the left foot as the downswing starts. At contact the weight is on, but not necessarily over, the left foot. Often the heel of the right foot will leave the ground, with some toe pivot. The weight

The drive (side view)

travels farther onto and over the left foot with the follow-through. For hitting on the move the weight tends to be more concentrated on the left foot throughout.

A cardinal sin is failure to keep the eyes over and on the ball at contact and fractionally thereafter. The lifted head — arising from a desire to observe the target or flight instead of concentrating on ball contact — is a fruitful source of inaccuracy and of balls flying uselessly over the cross-bar when shooting. Sound technique ensures accuracy.

There is no need to watch the flight or target.

● **Power.** This is derived from the co-ordination of many factors. These include body momentum (see Penalty Corners – In Attack, p. 129) and correct weight transference; bodily strength, especially of shoulders and arms; the speed and particularly acceleration of the downswing; and the locking of the wrists — facilitated by squeezing the stick hard — at contact.

The bracing of the left side at contact also helps. The maxim is 'hit into your left side'. It also prevents mowing or scything.

Driving on the run

Hitting to the left off the right foot – a more difficult skill

Opposite: The hit or drive – front and side views

Hitting/Driving to the Left

In all passing on the run, learn to make your stroke with minimal checking of momentum. Hitting to the left is easier with the ball in advance of the left foot. It is either moved there with the stick, or the feet are moved to the right of the ball.

Hitting/Driving to the Right

This is more difficult because of the greater changes required in the relationship of body and feet to ball. The fluidity of modern hockey requires all players, not just those usually on the left, to be proficient in this technique. The success of this pass depends essentially on the pivoting of the player round the ball with a strong twist of the torso, right shoulder pulled back and left pointing towards the target. Other methods include checking the ball on the reversed stick and bringing it slightly backwards (which may cause a would-be tackler to over-run). The ball comes into a convenient position, the body pivoting and the left foot moving onto the new line.

Alternatively the player may 'dance' round the ball, using a lock-step, left foot forward beginning to turn, right behind left, pivoting with weight leaning towards the ball, and then left foot on to the new line. See also Reverse-Stick Pass, p. 27.

Off the Wrong Foot

Top players can make all their strokes off the wrong foot. The hit is not the easiest and must be diligently practised so that it can be played when travelling at speed. For instance, in a crowded circle there may not be time in which to reposition the feet to shoot before a threatened tackle.

Variations

In the Asian method of using a shortened grip the hands are together but well down the handle. It is certainly not a panacea for avoiding 'sticks', but it may be very valuable for a rapid pass or shot following a dribble. See the photograph on p. 58.

Practices

1. Many of the push practices are adaptable. In the grid the range must be sufficient, i.e. at least 2 grids, 20 yds, after the elementary stage is past.

2. Stand in pairs and pass along a line for accuracy.

3. Divide into pairs of small teams, say 3 a side, e.g. A B C and 1 2 3. C hits firmly and accurately to 1, a suitable distance away, following his pass to join on behind 3. 1 hits to B and joins on behind A. A narrow 'gate' of skittles may be used. The exercise can be developed into a relay competition between pairs of teams. Accuracy and firmness of stroke are all-important.

4. This is a variation of no. 3, including moving to receive. The receiver must advance at least 5 yds to collect the pass.
This exercise may be varied still further if the receiver moves left or right before turning to drive to his partner. This practises hitting to left and right as well as straight.

5. Stand in pairs on a pitch 3 grids long with small goals at each end. Try to score against each other.
Vary this exercise by widening the pitch slightly and having two small goals at each end.

6. Stand in groups of 4. A plays shortish passes to B, C and D in turn. B, having returned the ball to A, moves off at least 20 yds. After receiving from D, A passes to B and all run to join B to repeat.

7. 2 teams arrange themselves as shown in a suitable area, say 3 grids long. X1 and X2 interpass briefly and then pass to X3 and X4, who repeat. 2 balls may eventually be used. Both the number of Xs in each box and the size of the area may need adaptation to suit the players' ability. Change groups.

X1 Y1 X2	AT LEAST 10yds	X3 Y2 X4

8. Arc of passing. A player should be able to propel the ball accurately through about 270°, though a push or reverse-stick stroke, as appropriate, will be needed for the sharper angles to the rear. Arrange tins or bricks around a 'clock face' and practise hitting them from the centre.

9. Players in 3s, passing from left to right. They should be approximately in line, suitably spaced.
A advances a short distance with the ball and passes left for B to

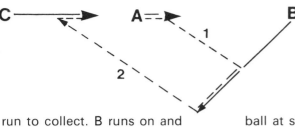

run to collect. B runs on and passes to C. A moves to B, B to C and C to A.

Adapt for right to left passes.

Reverse-Stick Strokes

Three reverse-stick strokes are covered here: hit, push and flick. For the scoop see p. 31. Sometimes the reverse-stick strokes are emergency strokes since greater power can be obtained by getting feet and body round the left of the ball to use forehand strokes. Time, however, does not always permit this.

In other instances they are valuable — and generally neglected — means of deception, as when beating an opponent or concealing a passing intention until the last possible moment. Lack of backswing for the short hit and virtually none for push and flick enhance the deception. The following points apply to all three passes:

● **Grip**: As described for playing with the reversed stick in the Indian Dribble, p. 19.
● **Feet**: In the normal running position. With practice all three passes may be made off either foot.
● **Body**: Inclined forward as in the Indian Dribble. Head and eyes should be well over the

ball at stick contact.
● **Ball**: About 12–18 in ahead of the leading foot when passed.

Reverse-Stick Hit

The short back lift aids accuracy. This contrasts with the high one invariably used when, for example, a LW tries wrongly to use a long reverse hit for centering instead of moving to drive on the forehand. The stick is swung across the body from left to right with little or no follow-through and is vertical at contact. The right side of the body is braced and the tensing of the right arm, with a staccato action, generates the power.

Reverse-Stick Push

Again the right arm provides the power but here it is supported by the left hand, not opposed by it as in forehand push. The blade carries on through the ball position, maintaining contact for as long as possible, as in the forehand stroke.

Most usually both hit and push are best played square or behind square.

Reverse-stick hit just after ball contact

Denise Parry, a great England forward, scoring with a reverse-stick hit. Note also the excellent position of the umpire, the late Jane Howard, whose ability I always much admired

Reverse-Stick Flick

The blade is in the same position as for the push but the ball is delivered with a flick of the wrists. This stroke has nothing like the power of its forehand counterpart. It is used for beating opponents at close quarters—e.g. to raise the ball over a stick or foot—as well as for passing. It can be played with the ball somewhat to the left of the body.

The flick is directed at an angle to the right, or ahead.

Practices

Although these strokes are essentially for use when moving at pace, start at the halt and then progress to walking.

A number of practices for their forehand equivalents may be adapted.

The Flick

As the flick is so closely related to the push, many of the comments made there apply here.

Although the approach to both is similar, the flick differs from the push in that the ball is deliberately lifted off the ground by the action of the right wrist. When used as a pass its best height is about one foot in the air. For shooting its value lies in its speed, the lack of preparatory movement, the controlled lifting of the ball and the deception in direction which is possible. Still greater height, as for aerial passing, may be obtained by dropping the right knee.

- **Grip, Stance and Body.** As for the push. For the lofted flick, however, the body at the start is much farther back.
- **Ball.** Level with or just in advance of the left foot, though this may be varied for short lateral flicks.
- **Stroke.** Begins like the push. At contact the blade is wrapped round the ball, which is then despatched with a flicking action. It has been described as 'Open the door and push'. A spring-like effect is obtained by the opposite actions of the two hands, right pushing forward and left back. It is important that the blade is not merely laid back under the ball to produce a sort of hybrid scoop. This may be useful, for instance, in lifting the ball over

The flick

Running into the flick

The aerial (lofted) flick

an opponent's stick, but it is not a substitute for the true flick.

- **Power.** Whilst this is basically obtained as in the push, much more depends on the strength of right hand, wrist and forearm.
- **Follow-through.** Again provides direction, and ensures that power is maintained for as long as possible.

Flicking on the run is much more difficult than with the push because of the special 'wrapping' action of the stick. It has, however, to be mastered. At first it may be practised by actually stopping the ball with the reverse stick on the run. Flicking with the right foot forward must be mastered too.

Practices

1. Many low flicking exercises follow those for the push.

2. Shoot against a wall with small targets marked at varying heights. Those representing the top corners of a goal are helpful in taking penalty strokes (see p. 138).

3. Rolling Ball. Dodge a skittle just outside the circle, left and right sides, and flick a gently-moving ball at goal.

4. For height:
a) A and B stand 20–30 yds apart, with C in the middle. A and B flick to each other above C's reach. Change places at suitable intervals or if C intercepts.

b) Stand in pairs across, or possibly along, the pitch, with A flicking about 15 yds in from the line (modify this for ability). B returns the ball from where it pitches, trying to lob A. Each tries to drive the other off the pitch.
c) See Scoop practices, p. 32.

Note

AEWHA and HA coaches do not use identical terminology or follow identical teaching methods in the lofted strokes. For instance, women coaches, unlike the men, lay some emphasis on the spin imparted with the flick. That spin does occur can be demonstrated by painting one half of a ball in a colour contrasting with the white of the other half. In certain circumstances the ball may tend to go with the spin into goal off the goalkeeper's pads. Men goalkeepers, perhaps because of the usually greater pace of the shot, do not regard this as a significant hazard.

The Scoop

The scoop is one of the two methods of putting the ball over the heads of players to avoid interception. The other is the lofted flick (see above). Its drawback, notably when played on the forehand side, is the necessity of preparatory movements, which telegraph the

stroke.
The scoop is played in three ways:
■ From the reverse side.
■ From in front, this being a variation of the first.
■ From the forehand side.
The essence of all is the laying-back of the blade under the ball, which is then slung or shovelled into the air. Generally greater distance is obtained on the forehand. *Confidence is the prime factor.* Because of the possibility of danger it is not a stroke for beginners. Experts play from space into space.

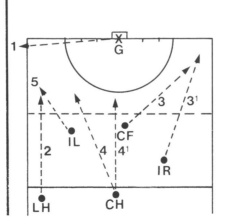

Aerial passing – specimen uses
1   G clearing safely into touch
2   LH to OL
3 & 3¹   Possibilities of passing to OR for burst into circle for shot or for a 'hook' (see p. 99)
4 & 4¹   For CF or IL to run onto – as against an offside trap or flat defence
5   Short pass to OL

Reverse Side

● **Grip.** Left hand at the top of the stick, with V of finger and thumb along the front, and right hand in a low split position.
● **Stance.** Body markedly bent and head and eyes over the ball. Arms and knees should also be bent. The right shoulder is dropped and points at the target. The right foot is in front of the left, both 45°–90° to the line of flight.
● **Ball.** Must be stationary, roughly level with the right foot and some 7–8 in. from it.
● **Stroke.** With its bottom edge leading, the angled blade engages the underside of the ball which is hurled upwards.
● **Power.** Is needed for height and distance. The maximum effect is achieved by:
a) Starting with body relaxed.
b) Transference of weight onto the right foot.
c) Bracing and straightening the right knee.
d) Turning hips and trunk to face the line of flight, bringing up the right shoulder. The strong lift from the hips may well bring one or both feet at least on to the toes.
It cannot be too strongly stressed that the whole movement must be *absolutely*

The reverse side scoop

smooth and rhythmical. Experts seem to make the stroke effortlessly. The biggest faults are trying too hard and 'snatching' at the ball instead of lifting under it.

● **Follow-through.** In the line of flight. Height is controlled by the angle of the blade and the lift of the follow-through.

In Front

This is, in effect, the reverse side scoop played from a different position, as would arise at the end of a dribble. In these circumstances the player stops the ball so that it is about 12 in. ahead of the right foot, which will be in front of the left again. The rest of the reverse side technique also applies, though in obtaining maximum distance the back and sometimes the front foot too may leave the ground.

Forehand

If right and left are transposed, the technique is very similar to that of the reverse side scoop.

Practices

1. See for lofted flick, p. 30.

2. If available, rugby posts may be used for obtaining height at different distances.

3. For improving accuracy and

range. Mark circles of 5 yds diameter – or squares of similar size – on the ground. Drop the ball into them, gradually increasing distance.

4. Start with one ball between three players. A starts with a pass to B, about 10–15 yds away. B passes to C, who plays an aerial shot ahead to A, who has run forward after making his pass. B and C move as shown. The diagram describes the sequence.

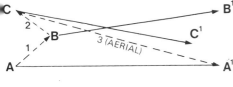

At A¹, A passes to C at C¹ to begin the sequence again.

5. Start with three players and two balls, A and C standing a suitable distance apart with B between them.

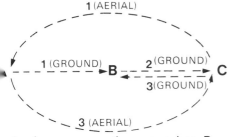

As A passes on the ground to B, C aerials to A, B controlling and ground passing to C. As C returns to B, A aerials to C. Change B as necessary.

Beating an Opponent or Dodging

Methods of what is known to men as beating an opponent and to women as dodging must be part of the armoury of every player. If goals are to be scored the various skills are vital; elsewhere they are needed to escape from difficulties.

By usage, beating an opponent has come to refer to the situation where the player with the ball has to eliminate an opponent. In this context it is an extension of the dribble (see p. 18). It should be realised that *an opponent is not eliminated until the ball has been taken or propelled past him.*

In a broader sense passing (see p. 52) often beats an opponent more easily than personally taking the ball past him.

In the 1 v. 1 situation two factors are paramount:

■ Control, which means a variety of techniques, not just a couple.
■ Confidence, which springs from control.

Techniques

The various techniques can be analysed at some length. In essence they all do one of three things: play the ball past the opponent's stick side (left dodge),

play it past his non-stick side (right dodge and reverse-stick dodge) or play it through his legs. Success depends on tempting the opponent into committing himself to strike decisively for the ball and then moving the ball past his stick. If he rushes in, the task is that much simpler. The one who waits is hardest to defeat.

■ Control

This has already been stressed. It interlinks with timing and enables the split-second chance to be seized. The ball must be kept very close to the blade until the moment comes, in those methods concerned, to slip it past the opponent.

If you attempt to manoeuvre at too fast a pace you will lose both control and the ball. Therefore, whilst every effort should be made to practise control at increasing speed, in a match you must not be over-ambitious.

■ Timing

The critical moment comes when the opponent is committed and is thus off-balance and unable to intervene effectively. Most likely it will be fleeting.

The preparatory movements must start out of reach of the opponent's extended arm and stick. *Commonly this distance is underestimated.* If, however, the attempt to mislead is made too far away, the opponent will have time to recover and make a second

Make full allowance for the reach of your opponent

tackle. The optimum distance is usually reckoned to be approximately 4 yds.

■ The Shut-Out

It must be made as difficult as possible for the defeated opponent to tackle back. Therefore, having rounded your opponent, you must regain your original line rapidly. Even if he is able to recover quite quickly, the opponent will face added problems in making a legal tackle. If the shut-out is combined with fast acceleration the opponent's chances are still further reduced.

■ Avoidance of Obstruction

At no time when the opponent may reach the ball may you interpose your body or stick as an obstruction. Avoidance of obstruction will automatically mean less possibility of any collision, which, however accidental, could critically impede your gathering the ball on passing the opponent.

Edinburgh, 1975. Janet Jurischka, England's centre-forward – her goal won the match – dodging an Argentinian opponent

Specimen Methods

In the simplest method, the ball is tapped or pushed past one side of an opponent – most usually his non-stick side (right dodge) –

Edinburgh, 1975. Anita White, England's captain, dodging another Argentinian by playing the ball through her legs

whilst the player runs round the other side. Or, if the opponent has his legs open, the ball is sent through them and collected behind him. There must be adequate space in which to regain possession before either another opponent can tackle or the ball can run off the pitch. A refinement, sometimes known as the check-dribble or pull-back, is to check

the ball, or draw it slightly backwards, on the reverse-stick, and, in virtually the same movement, to push it past the opponent.

Alternatively, the ball can be taken past the opponent on one side or the other.

Body swerves and other feints are invaluable in misleading and unbalancing opponents. In going

past the stick side of the opponent with the ball kept on the forehand (left dodge) a strong body twist with left shoulder leading is sometimes advocated. It has already been said that the opponent who waits is the most difficult to beat. To outwit him with the intention of going past on his stick side the complete sequence is as follows.

The check-dribble

At about 4 yds distance draw the ball from left to right with the reverse-stick, simultaneously throwing your weight on to the right foot. As the tackle comes in, transfer your weight to the left foot and accelerate with the ball past the right side of your opponent.

The feint must look genuine, as indeed it is to the extent that if the opponent does not conform the ball is taken past his non-stick side — the women's reverse-stick dodge.

The principles are readily adapted to misleading the opponent for taking the ball past his non-stick side.

Further methods include:

The Scoop Dodge. With right hand down the stick, scoop the ball low over the opponent's stick

The Jab. This is used when, at the moment of tackle, the ball has run a little ahead of the player. Hold the stick with your left hand at the top, palm upwards, and normally with left foot forward,

though it may be the right. The blade is thus also angled upwards. Dart the stick forwards and stab under the ball, making it hop over the tackler's stick.

Dummying. This is the name given to the situation in which the player pretends to hit or push the ball left or right. In the hit, pass the stick over the ball, just missing it. Having broken your opponent's balance you then take the ball past him on whichever side is appropriate. The same applies in the push except that the

◄ Beating an opponent
on his stick side

Beating an opponent ►
on his non-stick
side (reverse-stick
dodge)

stick is moved across in front of the ball.

Aim to sell the dummy at about the 4 yd distance.

Between Legs. This method may *occasionally* be used by taking the ball across the opponent's front with the *deliberate* aim of making him stretch wide. Depending on circumstances the ball is either reverse-stick flicked or pushed on the forehand through the resulting space — a most useful surprise pass, especially near the circle.

Note the defender's reaction to the threat of being passed on his right. The attacker has chosen to use a forehand stroke to put the ball between his opponent's legs

Opponents not in Front

Not all opponents to be eliminated will be to your front.

From Behind

You may be able to escape by sudden acceleration, achieved by

either lengthening your stride or increasing the rate of leg movement. Alternatively, it may be possible to check so that the opponent overruns and then make off past him, perhaps on a changed course. Changing course can also be used in the manner of the shut-out (see above), provided that it is done early enough so that it does not amount to obstruction.
Finally, you may accept the tackle, confident of your ability to retain the ball.

From the Side

Whilst 'From Behind' applies here too, another method is to check, outside the range of the opponent's stick, and then move off smartly more or less back along the line of his approach. In effect, the opponent over-runs from the side. This method emphasises the need for players to be able to scan widely as described under 'Dribbling' (see p. 21).

Additional Points

■ The Approach
The pace can be varied to unsettle the opponent. Denise Parry was fond of approaching at top speed, suddenly braking to invite the tackle, then accelerating away.
This fine England player also firmly advocated extending the

right forefinger down the stick to give greater delicacy of touch.

■ Improvisation
Many different situations will arise during a game, and it is impossible to deal with them all here. Intuition and experience will dictate how you should improvise in any given situation. Control will enable you to carry out the required movements. This applies not only to players attacking goal but to all others who may have the ball and need to avoid tacklers.

■ Encouragement.
Coaches should give this liberally to inspire the confidence necessary for attackers to eliminate defenders to provide shooting opportunities.

Practices

1. Practise side-stepping along a row of players about 10 yds apart. When the first player reaches the end he stays there, the front man setting off up the row. Players may scribe arcs in front of them with their stick at the full extent of the lunge (i.e. approximately 4 yds for adults) to indicate where the side-step should occur.

2. In pairs, e.g.:
X hits to O and follows the ball. O collects and advances to

beat X, carrying on with the ball to X's starting position and using the shut-out. The exercise is repeated.

3. In small teams. Each of a pair of teams of, say, 4 players, Xs and Os, stand at opposite ends of a row of skittles some 10–12 yds apart. The first X 'beats' each skittle in turn, passing at the end to the first O, and joining at the end of the Os. The first O returns, passes to the second X and joins the end of the Xs.
Any one method of beating/dodging can be done to start with. Later, introduce other methods. The ball may be taken on opposite sides of alternate skittles, on the lines of slalom dribbling. A competitive element – e.g. one pair of Os and Xs against another pair – is easily introduced but this should not be too soon. Spacing must be adequate and appropriate to the skill level to enable players to regain control behind one skittle before avoiding the next.
If, and in a non-competitive context, players instead of skittles are used, they may be able to offer helpful advice. They can also scribe arcs as in (1) above. As skill improves, the human skittles can indicate a tackle. Finally they may be allowed to become fully active.

Collecting the Ball

This section covers what is customarily known as 'The Stop', with the connotation that the ball has come from an opponent, and 'Receiving', with the connotation that the ball has been passed by a team-mate. As the game becomes faster, 'The Stop' suggests too static a technique, out of keeping with what is required. Admittedly the ball will often be 'stopped'; more often it will be merely checked into a suitable position for another movement to begin. When you collect a ball, you should always strive to know *before* it arrives what you intend to do. It must be one of two things: keep personal possession – e.g. dribbling away or dodging an opponent – or move the ball to your team's advantage – e.g. shoot or pass.

First-time hitting is often clearly a necessity, as in quick passing, clearing and shooting.

Nevertheless, in the defensive context of 'The Stop' beginners should from the start be encouraged to control the ball. Random first-time hitting may later prove difficult to eradicate and is dangerous.

Note: In many of the following methods it will often be advisable, for example to save time or to escape from an opponent, for a player to *move towards the ball*. This must be practised.

Grip for forehand collection from the front

From in Front – Forehand

Collecting on the forehand is to be preferred to the reverse stick since it allows the next move to follow at once if the ball is taken on the right of the body. Unless the ball is to be deliberately deflected or pushed past an oncoming opponent, it needs to be trapped so that it remains very close to the blade. From square on, turn so that your left leg is in front, aiming to collect the ball about opposite the left foot or midway between the feet. It can then be dribbled or propelled immediately. The right hand must drop very low, but *maintain a relaxed hold*. The left hand remains at the top, knuckles pointing forward. For improved balance the feet should be comfortably apart with back and knees bent.

An important factor in most collection is to *let the ball come on to the stick* rather than poke at it. To prevent rebound the left hand must lead the right, allowing the blade to be angled down. The ball is then momentarily wedged between blade and ground. The stick angulation may be emphasised on a rough surface. Alternatively or additionally, the stick may withdraw fractionally on impact to cushion the ball, rather as a cricketer's hands 'give' when catching. The head should be as nearly over the blade as possible and the eyes watch the ball.

The older method is still widely used. The same principles as regards avoiding rebound and the use of the head and eyes still apply, but the body stays square on the line of approach. Immediate distribution or dribbling is impossible and this method has largely been discarded in high-class hockey except, perhaps, when there is plenty of time.

On occasions the ball has to be taken wide of the body. The reach can be extended by holding the stick at its end with the right hand only. The same general principles should be applied as far as is physically possible.

Collecting from the front—forehand

Forehand collection at slightly different angles. Brenda Read favours a higher right hand

Allowing the ball to come to the blade, which is grounded

From the Front—Reverse-Stick

With stick reversed and right foot ahead, the ball is allowed to come on to the blade on the left of the body.

The stick may be reversed in one of two ways. Most often it is by the 'over the top' method used in the dribble. For a very rapid stop it can, however, be passed straight across in front of the body with the toe pointing to the right throughout.

Once the ball has been collected on the left, it must either be brought across the body or the feet taken round it—or a little of each movement—as it will not often be possible to play it away from where it was trapped.

From the Left Rear

The pass should be made so that the ball travels across the receiver's body, allowing him to collect it on the forehand, about in line with the right shoulder, without having to reduce pace. Indeed, it is better still for the pass to be timed so that the receiver may accelerate on to it.

Collecting so that the ball can be played away immediately

Collecting from the front — reverse-stick

As before, the same general principles apply, the right or left foot being forward as convenient. Sometimes the right hand grip may be strengthened intentionally to deflect the ball forward, though it is far more usual to need the relaxed grip and closed face of the blade. The closed face is of added importance if the ball has to be collected at full stretch.

An elementary fault is not having the blade on the ground. This increases the chance of missing the ball or of stabbing at it instead of letting it come on to the blade.

A ball from the left side is collected in much the same way.

From the Right Rear

The ball is taken on the reverse-stick, which may, however, begin to take way off the ball a little to the right of the left foot. This is an essential but difficult technique for any aspiring player. Men coaches, at any rate, hold that this method

Reverse-stick collection from the side

generally offers greater scope for dribbling and maintaining momentum than the alternative method. In this the ball is taken near the right foot, for which a strong body twist, with left shoulder leading, is required. The feet continue their running action, the ball being drawn forward to the player's front. In my own view indications for this are for a rapid pass to the right, when more power can be generated than with a reverse-stick pass, for a player on the left bearing in on goal, for instance, and when a shot is intended. Passes from the right side are collected similarly.

The Raised Ball

There are two methods: with the stick and with the hand (see Rule 12, I(e) and II(b)).

With the Stick

When it is possible to get the body on line with the ball, the head is over the stick which, well clear of the body, is angled forward by the left hand at the top with the cushioning, relaxed right hand well down. The stick may give to enhance the cushioning effect. No part of it must be above the shoulder (Rule 12, I(c)).

Collecting a slightly raised ball

Ideally the stance should be appropriate to the player's next move.
Sometimes the ball will have to be collected with the stick extended in one hand, calling for a good eye and fast reactions. The ball may be taken on any part of the front of the stick. If the blade can be angled slightly downwards it will help control.

With the Hand

Except for goalkeepers, who are allowed some latitude, rebounds from the hand are illegal. The recommended method is, therefore, momentarily to catch the ball and drop it immediately. Apart from the clasping action of the fingers the hand should be stationary. However the hand is used, it is important that it is relaxed and that the ball is allowed to come into it, thus avoiding any suggestion of a striking action, which is forbidden. So too are guiding and placing the ball.

Stopping with the hand

Practices

Many exercises detailed elsewhere automatically provide collection practices. In some, e.g. hitting/driving against a wall, a tennis ball may be used as it is more difficult to bring under immediate control.

Tackling

There are two methods of winning the ball. The first is by interception of the free running ball with no opponent in possession. The techniques are covered under 'Collecting the Ball', but a point meriting repetition is *the need for players to move to meet the ball.* The second is tackling, which connotes dispossessing an opponent. Even if the tackle is not directly successful it may still cause the opponent to lose control or to pass badly.

The various types of tackles may be grouped in different ways and, even then, experienced players will improvise to meet the needs of the moment.

Components of the Tackle: Mental

Restraint. Self-discipline may be needed to avoid rushing in to tackle. Attackers easily dispose of defenders who do tackle precipitately. Tacklers must generally delay their decisive movement until they have at least a better than even chance of gaining possession.

The one, and great, exception is in the circle, when every effort must be made, and risks accepted, to prevent a shot at goal.

Resolution. There is no substitute for resolution and determination to win the ball. Often enough, when

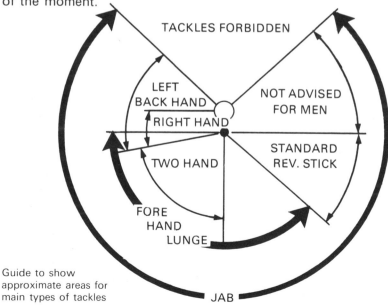

Guide to show approximate areas for main types of tackles

the first strike fails there will be the chance of a second attempt.

Physical

Timing. This is the essence of any tackle. The strike for the ball has to be made when it is out of the attacker's control, albeit only slightly and albeit only momentarily. It has then to be made very fast. Outside the circle tacklers must exercise restraint, waiting for or seeking to manufacture their opportunity. To do this they may need to run with the attacker or give ground as slowly as possible in front of him – but NEVER into the circle itself. These manoeuvres may involve feinting, trying to gain precious seconds whilst other defenders rally, and trying to shepherd the attacker into less dangerous areas or into positions more favourable to a successful tackle.

In sum, the tackler is trying to outwit the attacker, which is precisely what the attacker is trying to do to him. Body movements are powerful attacking weapons for unbalancing the defender. He must therefore *keep his eyes on the ball.*

Balance. Without good balance a player will not be able to seize the fleeting moment to strike, nor will he be able to adjust to changes of line and of movements of the ball made by the attacker. A feint will become a definite committal

and there will be no hope of recovering for a second feint or tackle. And when he does strike he will not be capable of transferring his weight correctly to give the frequently necessary extra strength.

Follow-up. Winning the ball does not complete the tackler's task; he must then use it to the team's greatest possible benefit. Whatever the circumstances, the aim must be to bring the ball under full control to make the next move with the least possible delay. Nevertheless, there will be many occasions, usually in defensive situations, when all the tackler *can* do is dispossess his opponent, having no hope of using the ball constructively. This is an emergency move only.

The Stance

In the traditional stance awaiting an oncoming opponent, the feet point forward, shoulder-width apart; the stick, with the blade on the ground, is held with the split grip, left hand at the top and the right low; the body is slightly crouched, square to the opponent; and eyes are on the ball. Since it is agreed that balance is a most important factor, it is argued that it must be adversely affected by the player having to crouch so far for the blade to be grounded. Thus the blade should be near, but

not touching, the ground and not so low as to upset his balance forward.

A further view in men's hockey holds that the player would be still better balanced if much more upright and that this posture would allow the stick in the lunge tackle to be 'thrown' in faster (see below). The importance of this factor rests on the fact that in fast, good class hockey this will be the commonest tackle made from in front, or approximately in front, of an opponent. This particular stance has been used in the lunge tackle illustrated on pp. 46–7.

The Lunge

This most useful tackle can be played in one of its forms from positions along a wide arc, ranging from the left front to the right rear of an opponent. It is most frequently made by lunging with the left foot towards the ball, especially when maximum reach is needed. It is essentially a left-handed stroke, for which the thumb may brace the stick, held at the top, from behind. The right hand 'throws' in the stick at the ball, returning to the stick for controlling the ball after it has been won.

It is also used as a feint when a player tries to trick an opponent into losing control of the ball. The illustrations on pp. 46–7

The lunge (side view)

The lunge (back view)

d

show the tackle played from the front. Played from the right of an opponent, particularly from his right rear, it is valuable for tackling back on him.

From square of him it is played as a backhand stroke; farther forward it may be played with either hand. From the right rear it will often have to be played merely to rob an opponent without, in the urgency of the moment, any thought of effective following-up. Generally, however, the ball will be moved only a short distance so that the tackler immediately gains *useful* possession.

Sometimes, when the tackler is to the front or right-front of his opponent, it is possible to adapt this tackle to a two-handed one. The left foot is again advanced to bring the weight over the ball, thereby adding to the power, but

not as a distinct lunge. It is then very difficult for the opponent to force the ball on through the tackler as the ball can be trapped very firmly against the ground.

The Jab

See p. 36. This may be played either quite close to the tackler or at full stretch and from a wide range of positions from the right rear of the opponent, round the front and over to slightly from the rear of his left, as the photographs above and on p. 49 show. This extreme position on the opponent's non-stick side is not, however, to be recommended for men's hockey because of the severe view taken of foul reverse-side tackles. Like the lunge, it is valuable as a feint. The greatest reach is obtained by lunging forward strongly on the left leg, with left shoulder and arm outstretched towards the ball. It is often unnecessary to make the ball hop over the opponent's stick. The ball is then contacted more with a pushing action of the blade which thus does not stab under it

Lesley Hurley lunge-tackling back on her international captain, Anita White

Reverse-Side Tackles

Tackling from an opponent's left is governed by Rule 12, II(c). The ball may only be played provided that there has been no 'previous interference with the stick or person' of the opponent. Coaches should enforce this rule. In men's representative play it is administered rigorously; any breach within the twenty-five by a defender almost invariably means a penalty corner.

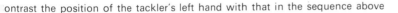

ontrast the position of the tackler's left hand with that in the sequence above

Standard Reverse-Side Tackle

By this I mean the tackle made with the reverse-stick held in the left hand only, left foot forward. The tackler *must be at least level with the ball.* Unless these points are observed a foul will almost inevitably result. Conforming to them ensures that, given a low approach with the stick, body and stick are well clear of the opponent. Timing is nowhere more important than in this, the most artistic of all hockey techniques.

From a well-balanced position as you run with, but slightly ahead of, your opponent, place the angled face of your blade on the ball so that your opponent over-runs. Alternatively, you may gently tap the ball or pull it slightly towards yourself.

Having gained possession, you

Reverse-side tackle

must then move the ball or yourself so that you may dribble away or pass.

Other Reverse-Side Tackles

THE JAB
As already explained on p. 48.

TWO-HANDED REVERSE-STICK
The photograph at the bottom of p. 51 illustrates this. It does depend on the ball being well away from the attacker's stick and the tackler being in front.

TWO-HANDED 'CIRCULAR' TACKLE
Although this tackle is not used by men, it was extensively used by women for many years. It is still sometimes played and has a special value for young girls who lack the necessary strength of the left hand to perform the standard reverse-stick tackle, a difficult one in itself. The circular tackle is also a good footwork exercise. As the player gains strength and skill with the reversed stick, she will come to use the other tackle more

frequently.
You need to overhaul your opponent. As you draw level, begin a strong twist of your trunk to the right. The left shoulder leads round the semi-circle, and your feet follow. This twisting action is very similar to the one required for collecting a pass from the right rear on the forehand. With the blade grounded and facing your opponent, judge your run so that you collect the ball as it is propelled ahead of her

Two simple practices are:
1. Start with two players. X, with the ball, walks forward with it, while O, the tackler, runs.

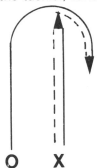

Having taken the ball, O walks it towards the starting line. X, having been dispossessed, turns right and

What do you think of this tackle on Janet Jurischka in an international?

Two-handed reverse stick tackle

stick. Continue round in front of your opponent, carrying the ball on your blade, still turning, if necessary through 180°, until you are able to use the ball as in Follow-up, p. 45.
You need neat, nimble footwork to move round your opponent cleanly, avoiding any interference with her or her stick.

runs to tackle O on her way back so that the exercise is continuous. The pace is increased as the players improve.

2. Start with three players. After A has won the ball from B, she dribbles back towards C, veering so that, as she passes her, C is on her left.

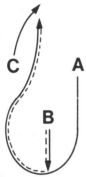

C then pursues A and brings the ball back towards B, veering as A did.

Practices

1. For left hand. As this is the more important hand for tackling, it is worth strengthening it and increasing its dexterity.
— Squeeze a suitable ball—small rubber or tennis ball.
— It may be possible in some boys' schools to play a great deal of fives, using the left hand whenever possible.
— Practice dribbling, moving the ball widely and changing direction and hitting with the left hand only.

2. In pairs. Tackler approaches from various directions. Each type of tackle should be worked up gradually, the player with the ball starting at a walk, progressively increasing speed as the tackler's skill improves. The player with the ball begins passively.

3. Dribbling and 'Beating'. Practices can be adapted by emphasising the role of the tackler.

4. 'Sweat-box'. The defender in a grid square deals successively with a string of attackers, each of whom he must dispossess before reaching the far side of grid (see p. 63).

Passing

Hockey is a team game. It therefore involves transferring the ball from player to player and the movement of those players. Tactics depend on passing and movement. Indifferent, not to say poor, passing is the bane of many teams. Nothing can adequately compensate for all the extra work needlessly loaded on to a team by one player's carelessness or stupidity.

Terminology

Passes can be grouped in various ways. For instance, in this book the following terms are used:

Direct. One delivered to the blade of the receiver who needs make little movement to collect it.

Through. A pass made into space for a player to collect. Ideally it is given so that he can control it without slowing down, thus maintaining the momentum of the attack and the pressure on the opponents.

Penetration. A pass which puts the ball round, through or over an appreciable number of opponents who are thereby, at least temporarily, eliminated from the defence of their goal. Elsewhere the value of the maxim 'Look for the penetration pass first' is explained. It is worth emphasising now, however, that much of the value of a flat cross pass is lost *unless the ball is then quickly moved forward.*

Square, Back, Diagonal. These all relate the movement of the ball to the pitch. Thus 'square' is about parallel to the goal line; 'backwards of' or 'behind' square bears its cricket connotation.

Reverse. In this much neglected type of pass, the player moves in one direction and passes back roughly to the area which he has left. It is invaluable in creating space, e.g. a CF takes the ball away to his right, drawing the opposing CH, then reverse passes for his IL to receive in the space so opened.

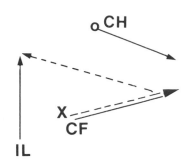

It is not to be confused with the reverse-stick pass, though this may also be a reverse pass.

Dog-leg. This involves another player acting as a staging post between giver and receiver. Thus, a LM wishing to cross-pass (see right) to his OR may find the direct route blocked by opponents or by his own men. He may then pass first to CH to transfer.

In another context it may be used as an attacking move, played from left to right. The diagram shows a typical free hit situation. CM holds his blade, slightly shut to avoid the ball bouncing up, firmly on the ground. LWB drives hard at it with

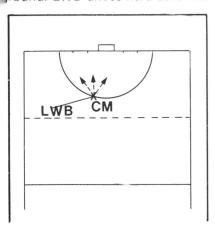

the idea of obtaining a deflection into the circle for a first-time shot by, e.g. LM, CF or RM.
Similar deflection type passes, though generally not to a firmly grounded blade, can be helpful in beating close marking.

Cross-Pass. A common and invaluable means of switching play across field. Pass 1 in the diagram shows CF and RM running forward to open space behind them for the cross-pass from OR to LM. Pass 2 shows a frequent Build-up Area move.

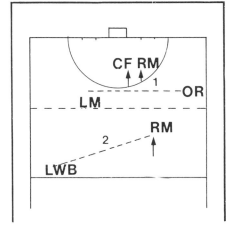

The reason for this pass is to unbalance the opponents' defence. If they are placed to meet an attack on one flank and then suddenly find their other flank threatened, they may need to make extensive counter-movements.

Furthermore, there are likely to be more players on the originally attacked side so that the switch offers better attacking chances on the other flank where more space exists.
When inners are using the cross-pass it is important for the CF to move forward to allow it to occur free from interception.

Wall Pass. One player passes to another who returns the ball rather as if it were bouncing off a wall. It is of outstanding use in 2 v. 1 situations; in very favourable situations two, and not just one, opponents may be eliminated.

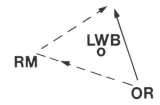

This pass closely resembles 'Triangulation', well-established long before the name wall pass became popular in hockey.

53

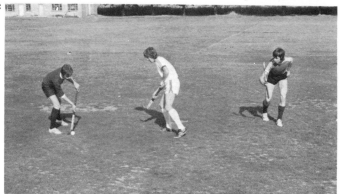

Wall pass

Timing is of extra importance in wall passing and triangulation, not least because when a back is being bypassed, there is often a danger of offside.

As will be seen, there is some overlapping. Hence, for example, a cross-pass could also be direct, through or square.
All types of pass have their place, for all have advantages and disadvantages. For instance, an intercepted square pass immediately eliminates two men, giver and receiver. The team overdoing square passing enables its opponents to concentrate too

readily. Yet for switching the point of attack, it can, as already explained, be a powerful weapon. The same sorts of consideration apply to the length of passes. A surfeit of short passes reduces the work load on opponents, permitting them to concentrate and cover without too much exertion. Conversely, a surfeit of long passes will almost certainly deliver the ball repeatedly to the opponents and give the forwards and midfields much needless running.
What is wanted is the correct balance in types of passes most beneficial in the circumstances of the particular match.

Components of Passing

These are:

Preparation

For the momentum of a movement to be maintained, it is vital for the player who intends to pass promptly to be prepared for his own next move before he receives the ball. It is said elsewhere; its importance merits repetition. Modern hockey no longer allows the time-honoured sequence of collect – control – look – pass.
In collecting the ball the body has

to be correctly placed to make the subsequent pass with minimal delay. Whenever possible, the decision on which type of stroke to use will have been made als Whilst rapid interpassing can be a powerful form of attack, it does call for considerable skill. When the passer has been in possession for an appreciable time before passing, it should be easier for him to achieve the best result, i.e. to give the *receiver* the ball *how, when* and *where* the latter wants it. If this maxim is kept constantly in mind it helps team-mates to look good and goes a long way towards turning eleven individual players into a closely welded team.

Accuracy

Although the aim is to give the ball to the receiver to suit him, nevertheless he is under some obligation himself to make sure that what he wants is in fact feasible.

For instance, if he is dead ahead and wishes to continue uninterruptedly forward, the only possible pass is an overhead one. He must therefore move diagonally off his line if he wants a ground pass.

If he moves to his left front the ball can be laid in advance of his left foot for reverse-stick collection; if to his right, then in advance of his right foot for forehand collection.

Whilst too many accurate passes do go uncollected, far more attacks break down because the ball has been placed so that the intended receiver has no chance of taking it. Accuracy also enters into through-passing to ensure that any existing gap in the opponent's defence is utilised before it is closed. See below.

Speed and Weighting

These are influenced by such matters as:

Receiver's Ability and Preferences. Some will be able to accept much harder hit balls than others, but all will want firm passes. Even so, it is pointless to blast short passes at the receiver!

The Gap and Available Space. These are inter-linked. With a through pass it is often necessary to find a nice balance between the speed with which to put the ball through the gap between opponents and the weighting which will enable the ball to lose way before it either goes off the pitch or reaches an opponent. A common mistake is to overestimate the size of the gap by not allowing for the reach and movement of opponents.

Having pierced the gap, the ball must not be travelling so fast that it prevents the intended recipient collecting it before it goes dead or reaches an opponent or allows him

no time in which to control it prior to being tackled.

Rather similar considerations affecting the gap obtain when a player approaching an opponent wishes to pass. Here the usual failing is to go on too far. Even if the opponent cannot get in his tackle, his reach — especially on his forehand — closes the gap which did exist when the passer was farther away.

Pitch Conditions. A heavy ground facilitates weighting by holding the ball. This permits more through-passing than, say, a hard surface.

Follow-up

Making the pass does not complete the operation. The passer must be prepared *immediately* to further his team's effort in the new situation.

The motto is **pass and move** — except in the rare instances when tactically it is best to stand still, as for a quick return pass.

Passing Practices

1. Any of the practices given throughout this book involving transferring the ball from player to player may be used.

2. A simple beginning. Three players with one ball. Free movement with interpassing. Some will consider this so easy that little effort is required. The coach will then face no difficulty at all in pointing out elementary faults! He should inter alia stress accuracy, knowing where to pass before the ball arrives, timing and weighting of the pass, and imaginative running off the ball.
Conditions should be applied as necessary: e.g. number of touches permitted before passing and varying distances and types of pass.

3. In 4 grid squares, 3 players, A, B and C, placed as shown, with one ball. Practise receiving as well as passing.

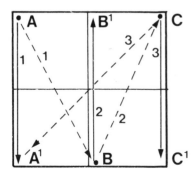

Sequence: A passes to B and runs to A¹ (1)
           B passes to C and runs to B¹ (2)
           C passes to A¹ and runs to C¹ (3)
From A¹, A passes to B¹ and runs to A
From B¹, B passes to C¹ and runs to B
From C¹, C passes to A and runs to C
Players may change positions

4. For long and short passes and timing of runs.

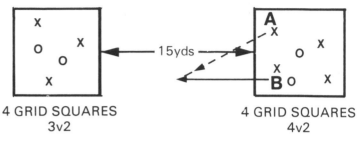

4 GRID SQUARES
3v2

4 GRID SQUARES
4v2

Set up with one ball as shown and start in 4 v. 2 box. The 4 keep possession until one (A) sees a chance of a forward pass to another (B). B then takes ball into other box, which becomes 4 v. 2, where process is repeated.

5. For long and short passes. Divide an area of about 20 yds by 25–30 yds (i.e. about half a twenty-five area) into two. Each half has 4 attackers and 2 defenders. One ball to begin with, though this may be changed to one in each half later. One group of attackers make a stipulated number of passes among themselves and must then pass to one of the distant attackers. Groups change round.

6. Possession Circle. This may follow more elementary practices of passing round and across stationary or rotating circle. Plenty of space. 6 on circumference and 3 players inside. 'Circle' may change shape and move about. The 6 interpass. Anyone losing possession changes with the interceptor; or change the 3 altogether with half the others.

7. Wall Passes.
(a) In 3 grid squares, end-on. A v. B starting near one end with one 'wall' man, W, on each side of each grid. A has to take ball past B to line PQ, using wall passes.

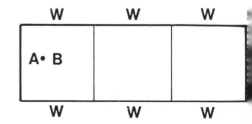

If B denies a W his half of the pass, the W returns the ball to A who uses another W. A and B should be regularly interchanged with two Ws as the practice is strenuous.

(b) Same number of grid squares as (a) with a team of 4, ABCD, at one end and a team of 6, numbered, at other.

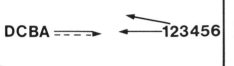

A advances with ball to be met by 1. 2 runs off to offer himself as the wall for A. Having eliminated 1, A passes to 3 and joins on behind the numbers, 1 and 2 joining the end of the letters. 3 now advances with ball to be met by B with C making the wall.

At first defender deliberately leaves open the passing angle. Later he may challenge or deny the angle. The attacker then beats him direct. The attacker is responsible for spotting to which side his supporter has run.

Scoring Goals

Everyone bemoans the dearth of goals in open play. Why are so few goals scored? It is recognised that defending is easier than attacking; on a given day a goalkeeper may be invincible; and teams may claim to have been dogged by malevolent Fates.

Yet these three reasons cannot be the whole answer. Since defending is easier than attacking then attackers – not just forwards – have to train and practise and work harder to overcome this disadvantage. Are inspired goalkeepers tested as comprehensively as they should be? What about the Fates? Are they or human beings responsible for the shots that went wide, the shots that hit the posts and the *shots that were never made?* Relevant factors include:

Mental Factors

Underlying everything else, attackers have to have more than a vague wish to score; they must have a burning desire to do so. Given this, they will then be in the frame of mind which expects to have opportunities. Open goals are rare, but they will now be attuned to foreseeing, recognising and taking the half-chance which, often enough, is all that may arise. It is quite correct to hammer home the fact that hockey is a team game but there are times when everything depends on an individual member of that team. That member has to be trained to recognise that critical moment. When it comes the player must have no qualms about appearing selfish. There is a great need for teachers and coaches positively to encourage shooting. *The greatest crime of an attacker in the circle is that of not shooting.*

Again, the apparent desire to appear unselfish may be no more than an excuse for shirking the responsibility of the critical moment.

The willingness to accept the responsibility to shoot cannot be divorced from confidence. Building up confidence automatically makes for the correct mental attitude. It can be engendered by encouragement and by the use of all kinds of shooting practices, a few of which are given at the end of this section. Confidence will also go some way to ensuring composure, despite all the stresses, at that crucial moment of putting stick to ball for the shot.

Physical Factors

Poor Technique

The greatest factor is undoubtedly failure of technique. A simple experiment will prove this. Split the goal up with tall markers or weighted lengths of tape or rope.

3 pts	1pt	3 pts

Any shot is better than no shot

The shortened grip for speed in shooting

Give players six balls spaced round the circle to shoot, scoring as shown. There will be few 'possibles' of 18 points. Players can be allowed to move the ball slightly if they wish before

shooting. It is unlikely to make much difference! Unless it is a gifted squad the results will show that the players are not as good as they thought and clearly demonstrate the need for practising accuracy.

Accuracy takes precedence over power, though in the experiment the shot, to count, must be firmly played. (In a match, however, any shot is better than no shot at all.) Technique may be lacking in aspects other than accuracy.

Because of the premium on time, speed in getting off the shot is important. Good footwork is vital. Even if shots will sometimes need to be made off the wrong foot, a player should strive to have performed his bodily adjustments before the ball arrives.

When to Shoot

This is at the earliest possible moment if the maximum number of shots are to be achieved. For the attacker approaching the circle it is when the ball is wholly on the line of the circle. As he approaches the circle the attacker will have fixed the direction of the target area. He can therefore concentrate wholly on his shot, preparing himself mentally and physically to strike the ball when it reaches the position of the middle diagram below.

STICK APPROACHING

CONTACT

TOO LATE!

GOAL

Drawing the ball from the reverse side to shoot

Selection of Target

Most shots will not score direct. They need not be wasted. The aim should be to offer a second chance should the shot not score. This may arise if the shot is on target. Some defender has to play it and, especially if under pressure, may make a mistake or there may easily be a rebound chance. Hence the importance of *following-up all shots.*

Hence, too, the shot over the bar is useless. Its prime cause is not keeping the head down. So also from a flank is a shot into the near goalboard or netting. The one aimed at the far post, however, even if going wide, does offer the possibilities of a second chance.

When time allows the attacker to pick his spot, and assuming he is centrally placed, he should remember that the goalkeeper will have most trouble with shin-high shots, especially on his left, and with flicks into the top corner of his stick side.

A special case arises when a player finds himself near the goal-line at a very narrow angle. (See diagrams, p. 60.) The goalkeeper's pads are blocking the direct shot so that he must choose the method likely to show most profit. If he is supported a pass into the area marked 'Shooting Chances' will be the answer, depending on the positions of defenders. Chances may also arise from a pass across goal just within reach of the diving goalkeeper.

If he is unsupported he has three possibilities:

- To draw the goalkeeper and beat his tackle
- To play for a rebound chance off the goalkeeper
- To play for a corner off the goalkeeper.

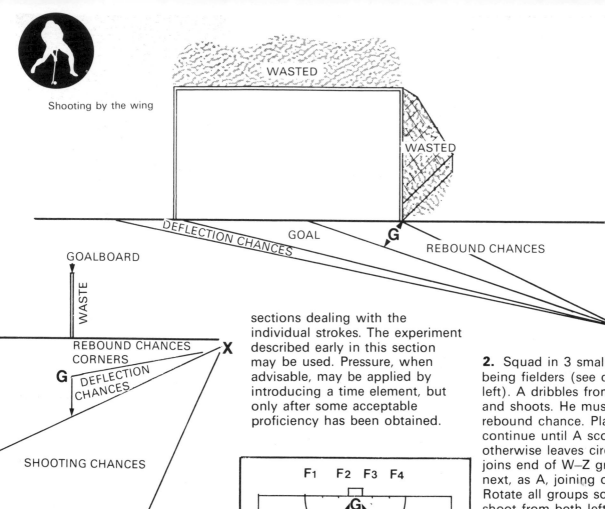

Shooting by the wing

WASTED

WASTED

DEFLECTION CHANCES

GOAL

G

REBOUND CHANCES

X

GOALBOARD

WASTE

REBOUND CHANCES

CORNERS

G

DEFLECTION CHANCES

X

SHOOTING CHANCES

sections dealing with the individual strokes. The experiment described early in this section may be used. Pressure, when advisable, may be applied by introducing a time element, but only after some acceptable proficiency has been obtained.

The one thing he must not do in either context is to hit the goalboard or netting.

Practices

A few examples of the many which can be devised are:

1. Stroke Techniques. See earlier

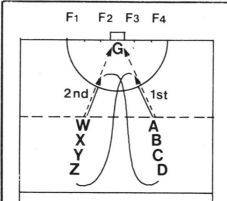

F1 F2 F3 F4

G

2nd   1st

W   A
X   B
Y   C
Z   D

2. Squad in 3 small groups, F1–4 being fielders (see diagram below left). A dribbles from twenty-five and shoots. He must look for a rebound chance. Play may continue until A scores or ball otherwise leaves circle. A then joins end of W–Z group. W goes next, as A, joining on behind D. Rotate all groups so that they shoot from both left and right. As success increases modifications can be made – e.g. goalkeeper may be allowed to attempt a tackle. Always stress that the earliest possible shot is needed.

3. To give practice to players coming from behind. Groups as in (2). A dribbles forward and passes to server, S, to lay off a pass in front of W, who times run to collect and shoot

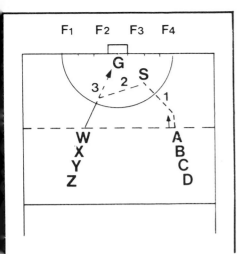

goals. Once round the pitch gives every trio four attempts and four groups can be working simultaneously. Each goalkeeper may have the support of another defender.

Montreal Olympics. Compare the straight-legged and stiff position of the Japanese with the much stronger, better-balanced one of the German

with minimum loss of time or to shoot at once. A and W — especially A — follow-up. Play may or may not continue as in (2). The practice is primarily for W's shooting and secondarily for A's follow-up. W should not be allowed to shoot if he fails to collect without a long rebound. Coach decides what he will accept within the limits of his players' ability. Groups rotate as in (2).

4. To emphasise shot and follow-up. Servers around circle with plenty of balls, serving only one at a time. Several attackers face 'keeper and 1 or 2 defenders in circle. Attackers must shoot rapidly from wherever and however the service comes and then follow-up.

5. Waves of Triangles. E.g. OR, RH, IR attack a goal and are followed quickly by another trio. Goals can be placed towards each side of the pitch on the half-way line in addition to the normal

The Bully

The bully, long regarded as a cherished characteristic of hockey, has diminished in frequency and importance. Nevertheless it does offer the chance of gaining possession and therefore the initiative. Any forward or midfield likely to be concerned should practise it. Customarily the centre forward takes bullies in the middle of the field, those elsewhere being taken by the nearest forward or midfield.

Rule 10 sets out the legal requirements. Much needless delay would be obviated if players always observed them carefully. The bully is played between one member of each team, with the stationary ball between them, each facing square to the side line and with his own goal on his right. Everybody else must be at least 5 yds away and nearer his own goal than the ball until it has been played. Each of the 'bulliers' then *taps* with his stick first the ground on his side of the ball then his opponent's stick *over* the ball,

three times alternately, before he may play the ball. The sticks must meet flat face to flat face.

Techniques

● **Grip.** As for the push, but as a trial of strength may develop after the third tap, a lower right hand may help.
● **Stance.** Feet apart, knees bent and body crouched forward to bring head and eyes as near above the ball as possible whilst retaining a strong, balanced position.
● **Gaining Possession.** The speed of the taps can often be dictated, though each player will seek to enforce the speed he himself wants. The essential point is to be first to the ball

after the third tap. At this stage the player may:

(a) Draw the ball away – provided that he does not obstruct his opponent's effort to reach it – then either pass or dribble away.

(b) Push the ball past his opponent, or through his legs, to a team-mate.

(c) Force the ball past his opponent's stick.

(d) Press and squeeze the ball up and over his opponent's stick.

(e) Deliberately withdraw his stick so that the opponent unintentionally pushes the ball to a covering player.

Cover is provided by a team-mate standing 5 yds away behind the ball. In the centre this is commonly the centre half or centre midfield. Elsewhere it may be a back, half or midfield. See diagram.

It should be noted that agile footwork is needed to retain possession and avoid obstruction, or, if possession is lost, to avoid the ball and to be able to tackle back on the opponent.

Practices

Players should bully against as many different opponents as possible. Thus a group may be split into As and Bs. After a few minutes the As all move up to the next B so that all As oppose all Bs.

In the early stages the opponent must allow the various methods of winning possession to succeed until some degree of skill has been acquired.

Other players can be added as the practice progresses. E.g. start 1 v. 1 with a bully in the middle of a small area. Then add coverer and perhaps another player.

Small team and practice games can be conditioned by, for example, awarding bullies instead of free hits.

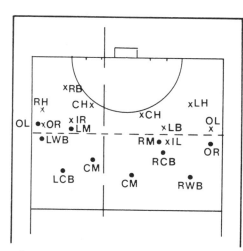

Covering at specimen bullies
Left: A wing bully
Right: An inside bully

The Coaching Grid

Although this book is not primarily concerned with coaching methods, some comment on the grid is relevant. The grid is simply a series of adjoining, suitably sized squares (not less than 2 by 2) marked on the ground.

Sides of 10 yds are the most popular for the squares, though they could be rather longer. If they are not drawn out, the corners can easily be marked by tracksuits, small blocks, etc.

They are of value in teaching and coaching large as well as small groups. Control is facilitated. Everyone can work simultaneously. The coach may thus concentrate more on what and on whom he is teaching. There is the incidental benefit of economically helping the coach to improve. As with all other aids the grid may be abused. Its very advantages allow the lazy instructor to indulge his vice. This does not, however, condemn it. Grids may be used to put over techniques, skills and tactical principles. For instance, the lines offer a ready-made check on the accuracy of a pair of players in an elementary propelling technique. From there the practice can be progressed into an 'open' skills situation. Gradually opposition, perhaps passive to start with, competition/targets, and supporting players are introduced. I stress 'gradually'. It is futile to

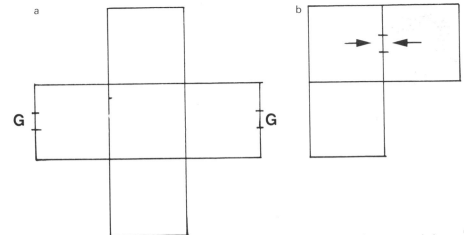

a

b

G

G

rush from stage to stage before the ability of the players is sufficient. One criticism of the squares is that players are tempted to perform in slipshod fashion, the ball being nudged rather than played firmly. The coach must be determined not to accept indifferent performance. In conducting such practices the conscientious coach will find ample opportunity to improve in diagnosing and remedying faults. Indeed the inexperienced will *have* to improve! In a 'keep ball' practice, perhaps 3 v. 1, for example, the coach must analyse *why* the passing broke down. To learn, the players *need* to be told why. Here sample causes are:

Passer – wrong decision – choosing wrong partner i.e. choosing the one whom defender could reach.

Receiver – faulty technique – failure to collect.

Third Attacker – failure to read the play – no decoy movement; allowing defender to mark him and receiver at same time.

The breakdown may have been engineered by the defender. The coach should be quick to praise him for it.

For practices involving more than small groups – maximum about 4 players – at least a second square should be added. I favour this for hitting exercises almost from the start. More than one square will be required for coaching such items as penetration, width, etc.

Nor should the coach ignore irregular shaped areas. See above. Small teams play against each other defending one of the narrow goals, G, in diagram a. Passes across out of bounds areas are allowed. In diagram b goals are scored by either team from either side. Such shapes encourage some imagination in passing and, at the very least, introduce a little, but not pointless, light-hearted relief. Grids are also used in a third way. They allow sustained pressure to be put on a man in a square, called a 'sweat-box' because of the amount of the activity he undertakes.

The player concerned may need to improve, say, his reverse-stick tackle. A succession of opponents are unleashed in turn across his square. He must win the ball before they reach the far side. They are not allowed to go over the sides of the box. The coach should maintain a rapid tempo throughout – which demands sufficient balls – but must give the tackler a fair, though not unduly long, time to recover to his starting position.

Although in this particular instance the exercise is primarily for the tackler, the others also benefit. The coach must therefore be able to diagnose not only why the tackler fails against certain opponents but why certain other opponents fail against the tackler.

The sweat-box emphasises perhaps the greatest advantage of the grids: the opportunity of players to make ball contact many times in a very short spell. A word of warning, however. If improvement of skill is the principal or only aim, the man in the box, and especially early on, should be kept there for a very brief period. His skill level will soon begin to decline.

Specimen Practices

Grid practices are very numerous. Coaches should devise their own. For ready reference here are a few suggestions in addition to those mentioned elsewhere in the book. They are not in any set order.

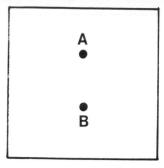

Practice 1. Shadow play. A, with ball, has to shake off B and place ball on either side-line before B can put foot there. No tackling

Practice 2. Play hockey, each trying to put ball on other's line

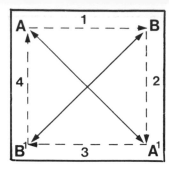

Practice 4. As 3 except both run diagonally. Ball moves round square. In 3 and 4 ball may be passed in the opposite direction for reverse-stick passing practices

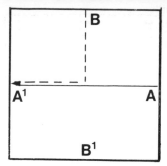

Practice 6. A runs to A¹, collecting pass from B in centre of square. B runs to B¹, collecting pass from A¹ in centre.

Direction can be changed similar to Practice 5

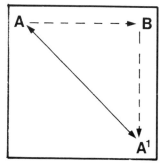

Practice 3. A passes to B and runs to A¹ to receive B's pass. A returns ball to B and runs back to A

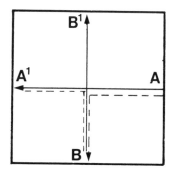

Practice 5. A crosses square, passing to B who runs to B¹, passing to A¹. All passes from centre of square. A¹ returns to A, passing to B¹, and B¹ to B passing to A.

Direction can be changed by starting with players at A¹ and B¹

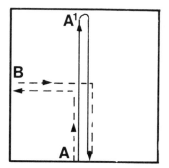

Practice 7. A runs, B is stationary. A with ball passes it from centre to B, continuing to run to A¹, returning immediately. He collects B's pass and takes ball to A.

For reverse-stick passing and forehand collection start at A¹

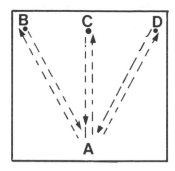

Practice 8. Target Man, simplest version. B passes to A, who returns it; then C; then D

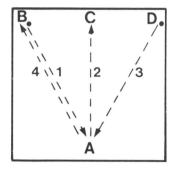

Practice 9. Target Man, more difficult version. Balls with B and D only.

A always passes to man without ball. Thus, B–A(1). A–C(2), D–A(3), A–B(4)

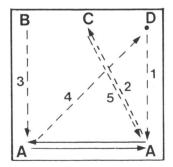

Practice 10. Moving Target Man. As 9, except that A shuttles back and forth to A¹, receiving only at A and A¹. Start from A to collect at A¹

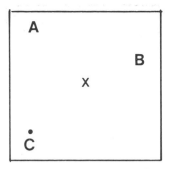

Practice 11. Possession Hockey or Keep Ball. How many consecutive passes can A, B and C make without ball going out or X intercepting?

When passing breaks down X takes place of last player of ball.

No tackling, A, B and C move and are not allowed to remain in corners of square

Practice 12. As 11, but with more players, extending area as appropriate

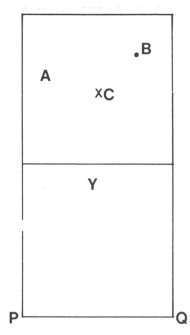

Practice 13. For delay by defenders. How long do A, B and C take to reach PQ with ball under control? Use stop-watch.

This also introduces marking (as X) and cover (as Y). See Coaching the Principles, p. 92

Practice 14. Hitting and collection. G=goal. A takes ball to right and shoots at B's goal. B collects, goes right and shoots at A's goal. Count goals scored in a given time. Repeat with players moving left. Aim to collect without appreciable rebound. Use for push and flick similarly. Flick, to score, must enter G in air. Flick also gives practice in collecting raised balls. Active or passive opposition may be added

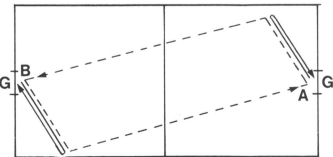

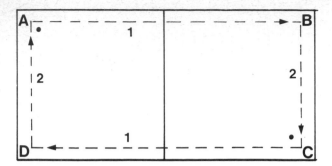

Practice 15. Hitting and pushing, A and C with ball. As A hits to B, C hits to D; B then pushes to C and D to A. Score one point when A has collected.
Variations. Introduce flick; and, for women, low scoop B to C and D to A.

Reverse direction of passes, C to B and A to D being made reversed-stick (short hit, push or flick).

Having passed, player runs to take place of man collecting

Practice 16. Dribbling. Select suitable number of squares, say 4 by 2 for small group. Players one behind other. At speed up long sides, jog down short sides. Forehand and Indian dribbling may be practised. With Indian, moving ball very widely from side to side may eventually be introduced

Practice 17. As 16, but alternating fast and slow on long sides

Practice 18. As 16, with passive opponents on long sides, leading to beating an opponent practices. Allow sufficient space between opponents for re-collection of ball

Practices 19. Wall Passes. Follows from 17. S=start and W X Y Z are the 'walls'. Jog first side. Give pass to W and sprint for return. Slow for next square, then pass to X and sprint for return. Jog other short side and then continue round grid, using Y and Z as W and X.

Develop, by adding passive opponents who are to be beaten by wall passes, when squad sufficiently competent. Adjust positions W X Y and Z as necessary. Eventually use active opposition.

Further develop by adding other 'walls' on the opposite side of players' path from W X Y and Z, so that passes are made both to left and right. Finally allow players choice of going past opponent with ball or wall-passing. At this stage number of players practising will need strict control. Ample space is needed

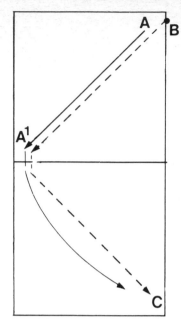

Practice 20. Collecting from behind. Three players. A runs diagonally to junction of next square at A¹, B passing for him to collect there. Having collected, he passes **accurately** to C and follows ball. C collects, gives ball to A and runs to A¹ to collect from A, pass to B and follow ball. B as A and repeat sequence

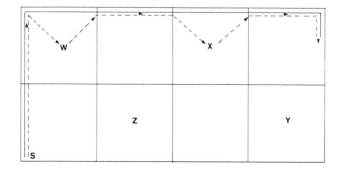

Techniques often have to be improvised in a match. Ann Whitworth push-passes for England against Wales with Valerie Robinson in the background

Systems of Play

The Playing Positions

Not so long ago, naming the positions was straightforward and the method well-known to everyone. Most present players have been brought up on the traditional system 1–2–3–2–3, shown diagrammatically as:

These are readily adapted to the 4–3–3 formation where the wing halves (WHs) drop back and the inside forwards (IFs) join the CH across the middle:

(GOALKEEPER) **G**

(RIGHT BACK) **RB**   (LEFT BACK) **LB**

(RIGHT HALF) **RH**   (CENTRE HALF) **CH**   (LEFT HALF) **LH**

$\left(\begin{array}{c}\text{INSIDE RIGHT}\\\text{OR}\\\text{RIGHT INNER}\end{array}\right)$ **IR/RI** $\left(\begin{array}{c}\text{INSIDE LEFT}\\\text{OR}\\\text{LEFT INNER}\end{array}\right)$ **IL/LI**

$\left(\begin{array}{c}\text{OUTSIDE RIGHT}\\\text{or}\\\text{RIGHT WING}\end{array}\right)$ **OR/RW** (CENTRE FORWARD) **CF** $\left(\begin{array}{c}\text{OUTSIDE LEFT}\\\text{OR}\\\text{LEFT WING}\end{array}\right)$ **OL/LW**

G

RH   RB   LB   LH

IR   CH   IL

OR   CF   OL

All systems spring from soccer, *even the traditional*. Soccer now has a range of names which can confuse those not familiar with them. In that game, 2-back formations are outmoded. In hockey the old basic formation of out-players of 2–3–2–3 is still widely used — albeit with modifications to its traditional method of operation since the change in the offside rule — adding further complications.

Whilst not everyone will favour my scheme in this book, each position is defined in relation to types of formation. The out-players are as shown below.

Note:

Although there are exceptions, as when making points on specific positions, in most of the diagrams no one system of play has been assumed. Thus IL in one diagram may be labelled LM in another, or, if particularly referring to women players, LI.

This is deliberate. It emphasises that it is not the name of the position but the player himself or herself who matters most. It will also encourage a breadth and flexibility of outlook amongst readers.

Essentials

A great deal of rubbish is talked about systems. It stems from lack of understanding or ignorance. It is essential to grasp the following points:

- There is no magical combination of numbers, the way in which systems are most usually described, which commands success.
- Any system is no more, and should be no less, than an attempt to deploy the best ten available out-players to ensure success in a given match.
- Any system may be played in

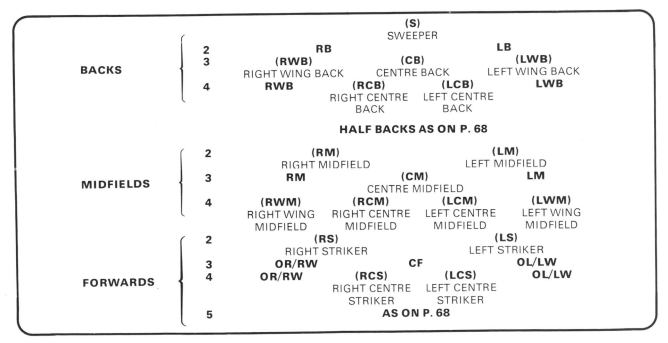

various ways, dependent on what duties are laid down for each individual player (role assignment).

Background

Some knowledge of the evolution of systems is necessary to understand them, involving an incursion into soccer history. (Space allows only the briefest resumé. For more detail, study: *F.A. Guide to Training and Coaching* – Allen Wade (Heinemann) *Understanding Soccer Tactics* – Conrad Lodziak (Faber) *Soccer Tactics* – Bernard Joy (Phoenix House).)

Soccer systems are described from rear to front. As hockey systems are derived from them, it is sensible to use the same method instead of the earlier, reverse, one.

Attacking Centre-Half (ACH) System

As more passing was introduced, the ACH system, with its balance between 'attackers' and 'defenders', arose from the early rugger-pack type play. This system, though some hockey players still do not realise it *is* a system, held almost undisputed sway in hockey for

about sixty years: one goalkeeper, two backs, three halves and five forwards. Described numerically it was 2–3–5, the goalkeeper usually being omitted.

Consider the accuracy of that. To give depth to the attack, and because their functions were more defensive than those of the other forwards, the insides played behind them, forming a loose W. *Thus 2–3–2–3 is more accurate,* a fact often overlooked by those who see no value in any alternative formation.

The ACH began to die in soccer when in 1925 the offside law was changed, making two instead of three the critical number of defenders.

WM or Defensive Centre-Half (DCH) System

A central attacker, well upfield, but now onside, posed a dangerous threat to goal. The CH therefore withdrew to mark him as a third and centre back (DCH). Previously he had been expected both to mark the CF and to attack – one weakness of the ACH system.

Another was the long switching movements necessitated by the dual role of the backs: to mark the IFs, yet cover each other. Farther upfield the defensive task of the inners was to mark their

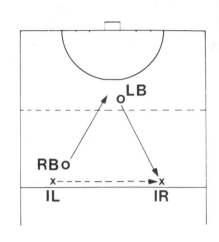

Traditional switching of backs
As IL passes to IR, LB is required to move out of his covering position to challenge. At the same time RB has to sprint at top speed to cover, leaving IL unmarked if the ○ IR cannot take over

opposing IFs. With both inners up attacking this was often impossible. Thus a third defensive weakness of the old system was the freedom afforded to those attackers. As against that, its attacking strength lay in the pyramid of

CH

IR   IL

OR   CF   OL

In **WM** the WHs moved in onto the IFs leaving the now WBs to take the WFs. The name arose from the theoretical disposition of

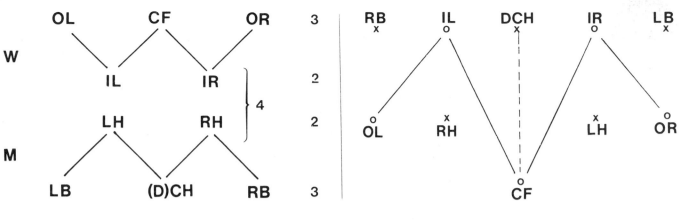

The **WM**

OL	CF	OR	3
IL	IR	}	2
LH	RH	4	2
LB	(D)CH	RB	3

Demolishing the **WM**

```
RB      IL      DCH      IR      LB
x       o        x        o      x

  o        x              x        o
  OL       RH             LH       OR

                    o
                    CF
```

the five attackers and five defenders, as shown above. It was described numerically as 3–4–3 or 3–2–2–3, the two sets of figures immediately casting doubt on the value of using numbers. *In fact they are no more than a convention.* The WBs pivoted on the CB (DCH) to give depth in defence and the WHs linked them with the forwards.

Countering the WM

The DCH proved formidable. The tactical basis of the plan which demolished him was to deploy the forwards in space away from the defenders' M, becoming an M themselves.

The deep CF put the DCH in a cleft stick. Should he follow the CF and leave the middle open, or should he stay back and leave his opponent free? The CF also linked with RH in the counter-attack. In addition a good deal of passing was played deep, luring out defenders to exploit space behind them. (See also Withdrawn Wing(s), p. 73.)

This presaged 4–2–4.

4–2–4

Facing the two advanced central attackers, teams added a fourth defender to make two CBs. Two links remained and the two central attackers could overcome a single CB. In theory six attacked and six, plus GK, defended. As WM, 4–2–4 in turn was over-enthusiastically adopted as a tactical panacea often without regard for the ability of the available players. Nevertheless a rear element of four still is very popular, many considering them the minimum of principal defenders. Some play one CB permanently in front of the other.

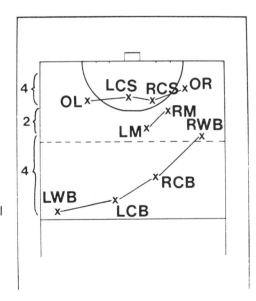

4–2–4: Attack
A specimen deployment for an attack on the right

Marietta Craigie (Scotland) shooting against England

Bolt or Sweeper Systems

Various Continental countries began looking for still tighter defences, credit – if that is the right word – for the development of the most defensive systems going to Italy with what they called Catenaccio (Padlock) (see below). The underlying principle was the use of a back free of marking duties who moved across the field like a bolt, providing cover, and who 'swept up' through passes. Yet systems using a free back are not *automatically* heavily defensive. A system with one centre back and one sweeper need not differ greatly from twin CB systems. One of the earliest sweeper systems, known as Verrou, emerged in the '30s. Numerically it was described in the same way as the system which, before the change in the offside rule, had, apart from the traditional, become the most popular in hockey, 1–3–2–4.

In the Verrou, when possession was gained the two links were reinforced by the CB. When he went forward, so did the sweeper, who became the CB.

Catenaccio

Teams using these systems did not play to win; they played not to lose, a subtle and often stultifying difference.

Many formations were used, not all depending on a sweeper. One which does, and which is now very popular in hockey but fortunately *not played in the same way*, is 1–3–3–3. In the over-defensive context there are seven principal defenders plus goalkeeper. In hockey the same numerical system is played in essence completely differently, further emphasising that it is not the numbers that matter but the raks or roles allotted to players. It is worth noting here that the orthodox hockey team of years ago wishing to hang on to a decisive lead in a vital game had one obvious and effective method immediately available. The inners concentrated on neutralising their opposite numbers and CH became a CB. This freed the backs from long switching excursions, leaving them in effect as a *pair* of sweepers!

Other Systems

A great many systems have evolved over the last fifty years. Some examples are:

1–4–1–4

Four front opposing attackers presented no major difficulties to the defensive element. When possession was gained, the solitary midfield was joined by one or more of the backs, but he had to be a player of exceptional skill and stamina. The backs might

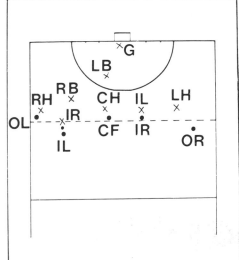

ACH System 'putting up the shutters' by using inners and CH in a predominantly defensive role with both backs free

find themselves well upfield and so able to join attacks.
With only moderate players, negative methods often prevail.

Withdrawn Wing(s)

A deep-lying wing may be used as a midfield to distribute the ball and to open space behind marking opponents lured forward. If both wings are withdrawn, the forward line becomes an arrow-head. Against four backs the aim would be to outnumber them centrally (see p. 74).
The free inside would be able to go laterally into the spaces, whilst

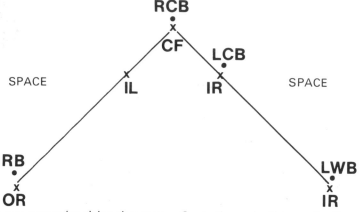

the CBs are committed by the two forwards sent against them. An alternative method is to flatten the tip of the arrow with both insides well up, the CF behind them being the one looking for attacking space. With only one wing withdrawn, the forwards may play in echelon, with the opposite wing and his inside partner advanced. In hockey, most usually the right wing would be up.

Such systems are most likely to work basically when opponents are enforcing a rigid man-to-man marking system.

From 4–2–4

The two midfields had very onerous duties. More and more it came to be accepted that another midfield was required. Most frequently a forward joined the link pair.

4–4–2 puts further emphasis on defence. The wing midfields or wing backs cover in turn the flank spaces. Farther upfield such spaces will be used by the pair of strikers to escape from marking.

Sometimes in this and other formations one man operates as a defensive screen or sweeper-in-front-of-the-defence. That is, he moves laterally in front of the backs with no specific marking role but with the task of picking up any opponent penetrating the midfields.

The most frequent line-up is, however, 4 (or 1–3)–3–3. In theory seven out-players can defend and six attack, though in practice not all midfields can be up with the attack one moment and back with defence in the next. Attacking play can be emphasised by encouraging any of the rear element to go forward whenever opportunity offers.

This general division of duties and the modified 2–3–2–3 are also the most used in hockey today.

Systems in Hockey

Despite earlier experiments here and elsewhere it was not until about 1966 that English hockey became interested in systems of play other than its traditional one. The interest, then virtually confined to the men, stemmed from the national victory in the soccer World Cup! At that time, and just as in the other game, far too often teams switched from the ACH system in the apparent belief that some other combination of out-players must of itself bring victory. Most failed to understand that players steeped in traditional roles could not overnight adapt to new ones.

Within a few years a number of European teams, taking a leaf from the German book, had switched to 1–3–2–4, using to the full the protection the then offside rule afforded the sweeper. It was usually claimed that this system spread the work load more equitably throughout the team. In fact the pair of links took over from the insides as the hardest-worked men. With both teams in a match using this system, much of the game's spectacle disappeared. Offside was much more common as the three backs pushed upfield, straight across the pitch.

In the diagram on p. 75, ●s have a free hit near the halfway line. Xs bring up their three backs, leaving to the sweeper any hit made through them. A mass of players are jammed into a narrow strip of the pitch. In such crowded conditions quite apart from the offside

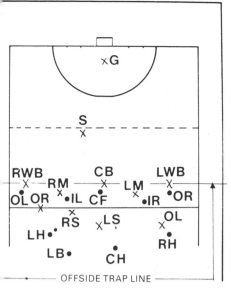

Typical pre-1972 situation of 1–3–2–4 defending free hit. Ball with ● LH

possibilities, many further free hits occurred from obstruction and 'feet'.

The fundamental principle governing the play of the sweeper was security. In face of forwards pursuing through passes or aerial passes – which, very belatedly, were coming into their own – he often had little option but to clear into touch, further disrupting the flow of the game and detracting from spectator appeal.

Considerations such as these cannot have been disregarded by the International Hockey Rules Board when, in 1972, they decided to reduce the critical number of defenders in the offside rule from three to two. After a few seasons the Women's IHRB followed suit.

By the time the change occurred, numbers of teams had had experience of systems differing from the traditional ACH. Though they had to adapt to the new factors, the overall changes were nothing like so great as they had been in soccer.

One player who was particularly affected by the new rule was the sweeper.

Previously able to play very deep, he now had to move much closer to his back line for safety.

More Usual Systems

1–3–3–3 and 4–3–3

At top level, the most usual system is 4–3–3, either with two CBs or one and a sweeper. At such a level role assignment may vary radically, the most dramatic difference arising with the sweeper. West Germany is noted for sweepers who have been able to attack at speed, threatening grave danger. Other countries prefer to hold the sweeper in a predominantly defensive role.

Advocates of 1–3–3–3 stress:
- There is minimum change from the 2–3–2–3 formation
- The attacking strength of the ACH pyramid is maintained
- Defensively the system is stronger than ACH or WM.

In general terms, tasks may be outlined as follows:

Forwards: Must be able to undertake much movement in all directions to exploit space and to afford each other mutual support. A great deal of lateral running is required in front of and behind defenders for these purposes and to unsettle opponents.

Their defensive duties include harassing opponents in the early stages of their attack and may also include tracking down their 'own' opponents breaking out. The CF usually does less of this, often being used as a 'target man' for long passes from defence.

Midfields: In attack, will support their forwards on the lines of the centre-half and inners of the ACH system. As their forwards may often find themselves closely marked, it is important for midfields to be able to break through to make man over situations and to achieve shooting positions.

In both attack and defence they work together as a team, normally providing cover and support for each other.

In defence the right and left midfields will mark their mirror images, e.g. RM will take LM or the player in that position. The centre midfield may operate differently (see relevant comment to diagrams on p. 77). Providing the backs are intact behind him and his flank midfields are positioned defensively, he may be

ree to move laterally in front of his defence to meet any added threat. If another midfield has not been able to pick up 'his' attacker, the centre midfield takes him. At times he will need to engage his opposite number and at others to take over from a back caught out of position. When this happens there must be a clear understanding with the free back. Although they do form their own little team, the midfields must also strike up close understandings with backs and forwards. Their characters and abilities will determine in large measure the team's pattern of play. If three defensively-minded men are in midfield their attacking potential will be far less than if there were two traditional insides and CH.

Backs: In defence WBs mark WFs and CB the CF, or the attackers in those positions. With their sweeper behind them, they are able if required to mark closely man for man. They may tend to pivot about the CB to give some depth. In attacks it is usual to allow and indeed to encourage the RWB to go forward either into the midfields or on into the forwards.

Sweeper: His duties are considered in detail on p. 103. Again, the backs and sweeper form their own little team, including behind them the goalkeeper, and working closely with the midfields, especially the centre, in front.

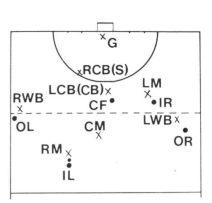

4–3–3 (or, in brackets, 1–3–3–3) in defence (1). Ball with IL. All five attacking forwards are marked with cover provided by the free back. CM has marking-free role in front of the rear defenders. Apart from supporting RM against IL, he would be on the look-out for halves, especially CH, or backs moving up

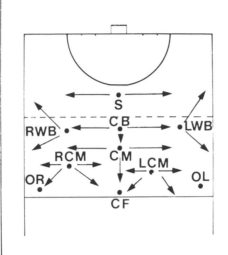

Intact 1–3–3–3 defence diagrammatically prepared to meet an attack in midfield

In 4–3–3 the only difference lies in the operation of the twin CBs as against one and the sweeper. Between them they mark the CF, switching between themselves, one up to engage and one behind to cover, as the tactical situation requires.

Some hold that twin CBs confer more flexibility than the use of a

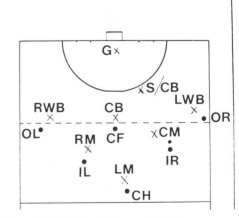

4 (or 1–3)–3–3 in defence, (2). S, or deeper CB, covers. As LM has not been able to pick up IR (with ball), he is 'swept up in front of the defence' by the free CM. LM takes the tip of the conventional attacking pyramid, CH. If ●s add a man over he will, if necessary, be met by S. It is most likely to be RH who should be tracked down by X OL

definite sweeper. As against this, an astute CF can cause havoc, given any hesitancy in the fifty-fifty situation when either back could tackle him but, just momentarily, neither does!

3–3–4

This system strengthens the striking force at the expense of the rear defenders.

Forwards: Do not operate in quite the same way as those in 3-up systems. For instance, whilst certainly not neglecting their wing players, whom they must also support, the centre strikers act very much as a pair. It is possible for the forwards to operate basically in either a convex or a concave line, that is to say with the centre pair either in advance of or behind the wings. If they are behind they will look to exploit space in front of themselves; if in front then they will look to exploit space in front of the wings. As a complete unit the forwards hope to deprive any opposing unit of four rear defenders of cover, a situation which they and their midfields would seek to turn to advantage.

Midfields: As in 4–3–3, with, however, an added defensive responsibility. As the backs lack cover, it is imperative that before the opponents can capitalise on it, one or more midfields reinforce the rear element.

Typically CM accepts this duty,

though it will not necessarily be he. He may pass through to cover the backs or he may take over the marking of an opponent – most often CF – so that the CB provides the cover. Plans to deal with such contingencies must be clear-cut and well understood. Confusion can be disastrous.

Backs: Mark as the three backs in a 1–3– defence and pivot about CB to produce some depth.

4–2–4

The backs operate as in 4–3–3 and the forwards as in 3–3–4. The reduction in the midfields places added demands on them. They have to undertake more lateral movement but always acting as a little team within the complete team.

For this system to work effectively, the midfields need to be of more than average fitness and skill at the level at which their side play. In attack they can be reinforced by a back on the lines mentioned under Verrou, p. 73. In defence they may sometimes need help from a forward.

In 1976 the women adopted the freer men's Rule 1 with relation to substitutes. Both sexes are therefore now able to replace a played-out midfield. The other method of relieving a midfield is to interchange him with a player from a less onerous position at an

appropriate stage.

2–3–5 (2–3)

This system played traditionally has been discussed earlier.

In a modified form it may be the best system for a given team.

Defence

It is as well to recapitulate the marking system. WHs take the WFs and the backs the insides, with the CF being left to CH. Thus the backs are not concerned with the central attacker. Teams playing this system *should* answer two vital questions – though often enough they go by default. First, what is the balance between the offensive and defensive duties of CH? Is he, for instance, to give priority to marking the central attacker? If so, then there will in effect be three backs. Secondly, how far upfield do the backs go to mark the opposing inners? A corollary of that question is to decide the defensive tasks of the team's own IFs, because of their responsibility for their opponents' insides when out of range of the backs.

Facing a fully developed 5-up attack, one of the insides may have to be quite deep in his own half if cover is to be maintained.

Half-Backs

To the extent that they link together the backs and forwards, they resemble midfields.

Defensively WHs act as the WBs in a three- or four-back system.

Supporting an attack, half-backs may obtain depth by diagonal play, pivoting on CH. E.g. with RH up, CH and LH would be echeloned back behind him. This, however, is only a very rough guide since often they need to be 2-up.

When upfield, WHs often tackle IFs to win the ball and maintain attacking pressure.

Forwards

Playing in the usual very loose W, the inners closely resemble WMs. The system aims to attack 5-up with the support of at least one half-back.

One practical advantage this system does have at present is that it is often the most convenient formation for scratch sides to use, since players have had a grounding in the traditional 2–3–5.

I stress that for the most part I have only outlined general tasks. Specific instructions to individual members, quite apart from their varying characters and abilities, can completely change the strategy of the team and their pattern of play. For example, one side playing with a preoccupation with defence would bear little resemblance to opponents with backs and midfields seeking every chance to go forward, even if both could be said to be playing the same numerical system.

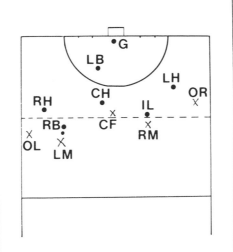

2–3–5: defence against 5-up. IL back to allow LB to give cover

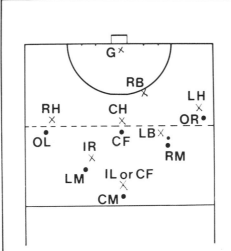

Conventional defence meeting attack by a 3-forward and 3-midfield system.
Now two forwards are needed to mark. Compare with diagram top right, p. 77

I repeat: *numbers in themselves are unimportant.*

Adopting a System

Too often a system is chosen for the wrong reasons. Thinking ought to be on the following lines.

1. Object

Simply, to select the system which will increase the *team* efficiency to the greatest possible extent beyond the total efficiency of the ten individual out-players. There is no generically *best* system, though there may well be one in the context of a given match and all the then relevant factors.

2. Ability of Players

The ideal team consists of only one specialist, the goalkeeper, and ten skilled all-rounders, highly competent in many positions. Few teams will ever be able to approach that ideal; most clubs will have to settle for very much less.

Even if they did approach it, amongst their out-players there will be inevitable differences, such as in physique, personal preferences and temperament. Nor

79

can they all be equally good in all skills or equally good in all positions. For instance, a player lacking shooting ability or the urge to shoot will be of little value as a forward or in a midfield role in which he will be required to come through into the assault.

3. Strengths and Weaknesses

Clearly there is a close link with (2) above. The aim is to develop fully any individual strengths and hide any weaknesses. Thus the fluent distributor of the ball will, other things being equal, be best used in midfield.

Conversely the player incapable of a high and sustained work rate would be fitted into other than a midfield position.

4. Ground and Weather

Such considerations may argue for the inclusion of the physically stronger player in heavy, taxing conditions, whilst fine weather and a firm true surface would favour the man relying on close stickwork.

5. Opponents

Though, because of late changes, it may not be possible to make a comprehensive assessment of the opposition, for many matches some time may often profitably be spent on evaluating their likely players.

The first thing to go for is any known weakness, e.g. mature backs slow on the turn and players with psychological weaknesses. Plans should be laid to exploit them fully.

Next it may be necessary to look at any notable strengths to decide if special containing measures are appropriate. It is, however, most important that any such measures should not be adopted, if at all avoidable, to the extent of upsetting the general balance of the team. It may be, for instance, that the team have settled into playing one system very effectively, whereas the opponents play another. This might perhaps indicate that three backs can expect to meet four forwards. This does not automatically mean that the team must of necessity weaken midfields or forwards to add a fourth back.

6. Role Assignment

This is the crux of the whole matter. Having outlined the general system, some variation, some particular emphasis in the individual tasks may be required. In the case just mentioned, it might be that to combat the four forwards a midfield – say CM if the team played 3–3–4 – was briefed on the early need in defensive phases to join the backs quickly. Again, given four backs, are the CBs happier if they switch in accordance with the tactical demands of the moment or if one plays in advance of the other? Or, if the opponents favour a free back, will it be possible to give someone the task of marking well up on him?

Clearly factors can change during a game. They must be recognised and dealt with speedily.

Minimum Positional Requirements

Notwithstanding the influence of the foregoing factors in determining the system to be used, those responsible for choosing sides need a framework to guide their thoughts. Three points require emphasis:
- *No* system will overcome the handicaps of sheer incompetence or lack of fitness.
- *Any* system can be played in a variety of ways dependent upon role assignment.
- The duties of players are not the same in attack as in defence.

In the past it has been customary to choose the out-players specifically by positions within the ACH system. This is far from ideal – as, too, is picking men for specific positions in any other predetermined system.

Circumstances may admittedly force this outmoded method on some clubs. Nevertheless, what is required is for those choosing teams to have in mind a framework consisting of the minimum number of players needed for the three basic elements of the team. This is necessary because if, for instance, and taking an extreme case, eight of the ten best players were backs clearly they could not all play. Views on these minima may vary. For example it is possible to work with only a pair of full-time forwards; the 1–4–1–4 system has been described on p. 73 in which there is only one midfield; and there may be just two backs. These considerations would postulate a 2–1–2 minimal skeleton, leaving five places to be filled by the best available remaining talent. Few, I imagine, would wish to work on that numerical basis. The important thing is to have some such skeleton in mind when starting selection.

The next stage is to select players for the underlying framework. Having chosen those players, the best remaining ones are deployed and the final system established. The following paragraphs outline my own preferences and give the reasons.

Forwards: One of the main problems in hockey (even in the pre-1972 days with the ACH system) is the provision of an adequate striking force. Notwithstanding the fact that midfields and backs are theoretically expected to join the assault echelon, I postulate three forwards at least.

Midfields: As they are needed to attack and to defend, there cannot effectively be less than two.

Backs: Because of the danger of an advanced central attacker, I prefer a minimum of three backs. If only two are used they will need a good deal of help from wing midfields.

Overall, then, in team selection I myself would be looking to work on a 3–2–3 basis, leaving two more to be fitted into the optimum framework for any given match. *However,* if for some reason sufficiently good players were not available for these eight positions, then my system for that match would have to be modified to suit what was available – a rather different and more flexible approach than the traditional one of looking specifically for two backs, three halves and five forwards.

Finally, note the use of the word 'framework'. A system *is* a framework, on which players should be encouraged to build with understanding and skilled spontaneity.

Numbers do not much matter. What does matter is that every player knows:
- What to do when he has the ball.
- What to do when a team-mate has it.
- What to do when possession has been lost.
- What his team-mates should be doing in these three situations.

When all the players do know all these answers they *understand* their system; without this understanding they cannot develop its full potential.

Whither Systems?

Within the last couple of years the phrase 'total football' has come to the fore in soccer. It has evoked a reverence worthy of a revelation. It does have value, but does not have novelty! Long ago, the name 'the Whirl' was coined for much the same sort of philosophy – a constant rotation of players all able to play in any of the out-positions.

By comparison, hockey with its strangely shaped club and small ball is a much more difficult game. It will take longer, for instance, for RWBs to be competent OLs. Yet, as I have already indicated, this is the way ahead. Children need to be brought up primarily to be skilled hockey players. Specialisation should be given far less importance. For one thing, it may emerge spontaneously from personal preferences and inclinations. For another, a team of one-position specialists will have only limited tactical scope. In the future no player should be called a 'good' CH, CB, etc. unless he is basically an able player in every element of the team. This presupposes automatically an understanding of the methods of play used in those elements. If, now, the player has the skills and the understanding, he must have the speed and stamina which will enable him to appear in many different positions during the course of a game. These four fundamentals offer the greatest hope of teams driven back on the defensive being able to break out in force, as opposed to mere raids, to pose sustained threats to their opponents' goal.

England forward Elizabeth Boobier in action against Wales

Tactical Fundamentals

The principles upon which tactics are based may be analysed in various ways. Whatever scheme is adopted the aim is constant: to produce a side playing as an efficient and completely integrated unit, the successful *team*.

Integration

Integration, the conception of the 'oneness' of a team, whatever the phase of play, is fundamental to all tactical principles. Just which is the phase of play at any given moment depends upon ball possession. Put quite simply: when any member of the team has the ball *every* member is attacking; and when their opponents have the ball *every* member of the team is defending. Over the last ten years this concept has become more widely understood in English hockey. Nevertheless, in many instances it is not so, or the implications are not appreciated. Unless all players do fully grasp this, they cannot be in the right frame of mind to react with optimum effect on their team's effort. Nor, when possession changes, will they be able to react at the speed required by the pace of modern hockey.

Other Principles

Diagrammatically, the whole scheme of principles which I have chosen to use *as appropriate to this book* may be shown thus:

Each principle interlocks with the others in its set. Each set aims at achieving tactical success over the other. Sometimes there will be a clash of an individual principle with another in the same set. One of the commonest in the attack is to give support to the man with the ball and to maintain width at the same time. In the orthodox W the IFs may be deep in their own half, some distance from their other forwards.

INTEGRATION

ATTACK (with possession)	DEFENCE (without possession)
Aim: to score	Aim: to regain possession
DEPTH	SECURITY
SUPPORT	CONCENTRATION
WIDTH	DEPTH
MOBILITY	SUPPORT
PENETRATION	DELAY

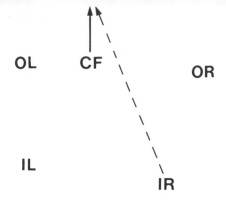

Here IR has won the ball and passed it to CF. Only OL and OR are in supporting range of CF. What do they do? Do they move to his support and sacrifice width or do they maintain width and leave him unaided?

Many tactical problems which arise can only be solved by players' experience and insight. The correct solution usually depends on evaluating three factors:

■ position of the ball
■ position of team-mates
■ position of opponents
and making appropriate allowance for movement.

Here, only the three front forwards are capable of influencing the play in the near term. Much will depend on the positions and movements of opponents. For instance, against a firmly held middle, the CF may wish to use a wing to outflank it. Another possibility is that the CF has a clear run into the circle for a shot, in which event the wings will come in looking for rebound chances. Between these two extremes there will be many other variations.

Attack
Depth

By attacking in depth players offer themselves more passing opportunities, making things less predictable for their opponents. Imagine four players in a line:

Now move them slightly:

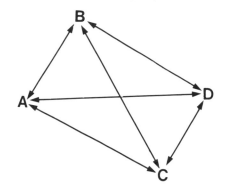

Passing possibilities have increased considerably.

The underlying reasoning here is exemplified in the positioning of players in 'The Hook' (see p. 99). For practical purposes three players are the minimum required to provide depth, and they must be in some triangular pattern. The concept of triangles forms one of the bases of both attack and defence. During a match any given triangle – e.g. a right flank triangle of RH, OR and IR – will change in

shape, size and direction. Further, its constituent members will also change. See below.

Support

This links closely with depth. Serious students of the game will find that not all authorities will list both support and depth as principles of play. It is worth noting that support does not necessarily connote *close* support – important as that is – and that support may well be in advance of the ball.

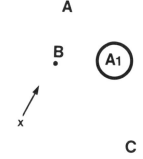

X is a defender moving to tackle B. To beat this tackle B has the *physical* support of A, who will immediately engage X if his tackle succeeds; but B also has the *passing* support of C, to whom he may be able to play the ball before X arrives. A rapid run by A to the A1 area would offer further *passing* support.

Whilst it is clearly desirable for an attacker to have at least two supporters – the triangle again –

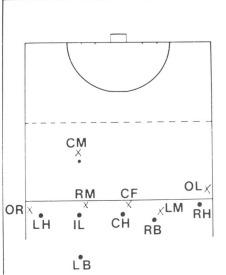

Support for their No. 7 from the New Zealanders – the eventual champions – in their match with West Germany in the Montreal Olympics, 1976

very frequently this will simply be impossible, as from a long pass in a breakout.

The rule here is that *someone*, whoever is handiest, does his utmost to race up in support. Rapid foresight is often necessary. Although *someone must* do all in his power to be within effective reach, sometimes no one can do so. The player with the ball will then have to assess his chances if he forges ahead alone. Against a strongly arrayed defence he must await the arrival of support, being prepared to withstand tackles in the meantime. He will probably move laterally towards the area where he expects support to materialise fastest.

Plunging on thoughtlessly will, except by great good luck, merely lose possession and, at the same time, involve other members of the team in fast running.

Finally, under Passing on p. 52 attention has been drawn to the need for the man making a pass to move. The first thought should be to move towards, not away from, the receiver. If *no one* moves towards him he will have no support. Moving towards the man in possession can be helpful in other contexts. Imagine CM with the ball with his attacking element in line abreast across the field and being marked (see diagram top right).

If some now move *towards* CM, their markers have to decide whether to go with them or let them run free. If they stand off the attack builds up without hindrance – possibly by CM passing and then advancing to make a 2 v. 1 on one of the markers; if they go with them

they open space behind themselves into which CM may usefully play the ball.

Particularly at club level, players are much too prone to do the wrong thing by haring off *away* from the ball.

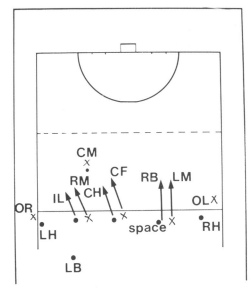

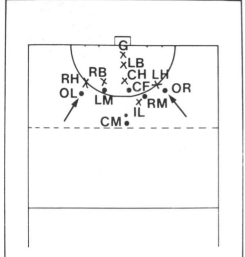

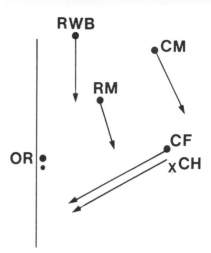

Width

Without the unintentional help of his opponents, a defender cannot simultaneously mark an opponent and mark (or cover) space. This unintentional help will not be volunteered if attacks are made on a wide front.

Since attackers can only score if they are in the circle, defenders will try to deny the circle, which means they will tend automatically to concentrate in the middle portion of the pitch. Opponents who crowd inwards facilitate their task. Wings, even at levels where they should know a great deal better, are the major culprits. It is all too common to see a CM in the type of situation above, made much worse by the misguided runs of the wings, who, directly contributing to the compactness of the defence, are expecting passes in hopeless positions.

In other circumstances it may be perfectly correct to come in. One example is quoted under Support, above. Another well-known one, especially against man-to-man marking, occurs when the wing does it with the intention of opening space on the flank for a player coming from behind – who re-establishes width.

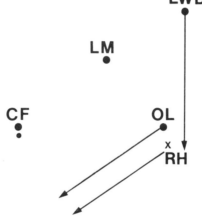

The same may apply when a central player moves out to support a wing, or to draw his marker from the middle. See top right.

I have deliberately used the RM to move towards the middle. A typical mistake in such a situation would be for the RM/IR to crowd over with OR and CF, despite the supporting RWB/RH.

Another elementary error arises in a 2 v. 1 situation when the supporter moves so close to the player with the ball that the single defender is able to contain both attackers.

Mobility

The correct way to run over a distance to allow free movement of muscles and lungs. Carrying the stick in both hands inhibits this movement, upsets balance and reduces pace

Mobility connotes much more than the ability of a player to run at speed whenever necessary throughout a game. It requires a tactical eye and versatility. Tactically players should think in terms of triangles, or at least of their operational or 'immediate' triangles. Taking a 1–3–3–3 formation some of these are:

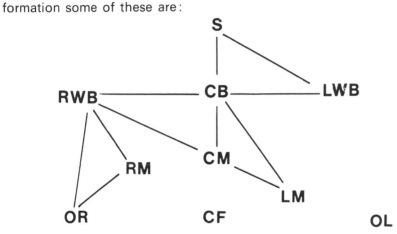

When a player has the ball the other members of his operational triangles should be thinking of what is to follow and reacting – as, so often, by moving to take a pass – to the optimum benefit of the team. More than two people are concerned because every player has more than one triangle. Thus if RWB has the ball, S, CB, CM, RM and OR are all immediately involved. Those not immediately involved should be preparing for the potential next move but one. For instance, CF should be asking himself 'Where should I be most useful if RWB passes to RM?' and equating the answer to that question with answers to others such as 'Where would I be most useful if RWB passes to OR?'

Ideally every out-player should be competent in the other nine out-positions. The practical minimum which clubs should strive to achieve is for him to be competent in the positions concerned in his immediate triangles. Thus, again taking RWB, he needs to be a competent S, CB, CM, RM and OR.

It is possible to draw in many other triangles to more distant players such as RWB–LM–CF, and frequently enough these more distant players will receive the pass. Cross passes from a WH to his opposite IF are traditional and strong attacking moves, for instance. Therefore, the players out of an immediate triangle must not only be thinking on the lines indicated above, but also in terms of finding space for receiving the ball direct. This is where, in assessing swiftly so many factors, the tactical eye comes into its own.

Mobility is needed to overcome well-organised defences. *Stereotyped hockey with attackers confined to certain areas will not do.* Generally what is lacking is *purposeful* lateral and diagonal movement, in front of, through, and, especially, behind defenders, with due regard being paid to the avoidance of offside.

Attacking runs more or less straight upfield or direct on goal have their place, and, at the right time, can be a vital factor. They need to be used with discretion. The organised defence will go with the attackers and stay organised. They will not find it so easy with cross-field movement.

Immediately, a marker has to decide whether to go with his man to stop him receiving a possible pass or whether to hold his ground to avoid opening a potentially dangerous gap in the defensive grouping.

Some movements, especially at free hits, can be rehearsed. Many more cannot. The correct, spontaneous reaction depends on the tactical eye – or flair.

Teamwork is essential if mobility is

to pay highest dividends. Often more than the man in possession and one man off the ball will be involved. The aim should be for an understanding throughout the team of what is being attempted. A simple illustration:

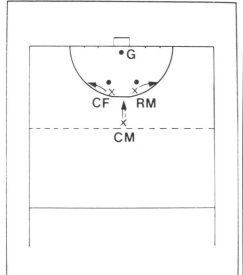

CM, bursting through, needs space in which to shoot. Both CF and RM must realise this and veer away far enough to be able to receive a pass should CM have to make it because one of the markers stays in the middle to block him, instead of following his man.

In another illustration on the same theme, OL attacking RH intends to beat him on his reverse-stick side. LM and CF move from the area into which the OL will come. Either may receive a pass if allowed to run free. Meanwhile, RM goes across to support OL from behind. Four players are thus involved in this manoeuvre.

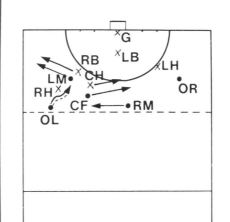

Penetration

Penetration means playing the ball without loss of possession round, through or over defenders. The aerial pass is of special value from the Build-Up Area for launching attacks. (See p. 31.) Looking first for the penetrating pass has already been advocated. Moving the ball forward promptly reduces the time available to the defence in which to regroup. In the situation below, ● RB, who has won the ball from X IL, could pass to either RH or OR. The first retains possession but nothing more. The second, the penetrating pass, puts the ball behind no fewer than seven opponents.

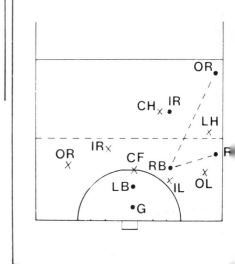

Players opening space for another have been illustrated. Similar action may be needed to open a path for a penetrating pass.

In the counter-attack it is particularly important to try to play the ball fast through as many of the opposing midfields — and even backs — as possible.

Defence

Security

This is the first requisite of all sound defence. Give nothing away; take no chances. The Defence Area is no place in which to run risks. Since the most dangerous part of the circle is in front of goal and since goals cannot be scored from outside the circle, it follows that in principle clearances need to be:

- **Swift.** The longer the ball is in the circle the greater the danger. 'Pretty' hockey or interpassing between defenders invites catastrophe.
- **Wide.** I.e. played out square, or only slightly in front of square, rather than diagonally and certainly not straight upfield. Goalkeepers often offend.
- **Long.** The farther from the circle the ball travels, the longer it will take to be returned and the greater the chance of preventing its return.

The twin concepts of width and length may need to be instilled into players. Some women goalkeepers, for instance, seem happy barely to clear the circle with a kick.

Clearances

Area b/goalmouth/c is the preferred, with area b/goalmouth/a allowing a margin for avoiding concession of a corner.

Area X is **not** to be used. The one exception would be a powerful and **safely** raised ball landing well into the Build-Up Area. The failure rate in attempting this is, in general, unacceptably high.

F and G are defenders. The clearance to F — wide and long — is, other things being equal, the one of choice

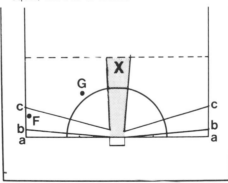

Only one word needs to be said about clearing across the field inside the twenty-five: **don't!** The possibility of interception is far too great.

Concentration

In its general aspect this relates to the coming together of defenders to present a closely-knit barrier between attackers and goal. The various triangles of the defenders will be interlocked, and space available to their opponents reduced. The defenders will be most effective when able to contain the attacks on a narrow front — hence, from the attackers' point of view, the value of width.

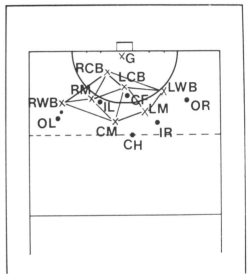

Tightly-locked defensive triangles of a 4–3–3 near and in their circle

In a more particular sense, concentration refers to movement to meet the immediate or main threat. If it occurs with the defence outnumbered it will be necessary to leave the least dangerous opponent open. With the straightforward case of 2 v. 1 outside the circle, the single defender has to try to defeat

Holland 'concentrating' against India at Montreal. Goalkeepers – note the Dutchman's equipment. Umpires – note the position of Graham Nash (England), who is well able to see everything

have sufficient time in which to adjust to the new threat.
Other defensive switching may not need to be so extreme. In more favourable circumstances, for instance, it might be feasible for LB to intercept OR whilst the defeated LH picked up IR.

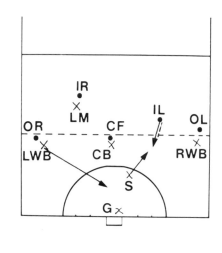

both opponents, if at all possible, or at least delay them until support arrives. This would preferably be another out-player but might have to be the goalkeeper. The defender's prime concern, however, must be the man who has the ball, not the one who *may* receive it. It would be plainly ridiculous to stand off the player in possession in anticipation of a pass, so giving him free passage into the circle for a shot.
More complicated cases involve numbers of defenders, the classic one being when, in a 2–3– system, an opposing wing has eliminated his marking half-back.
In the first diagram, Xs are in trouble. ● OR has eliminated LH and has left LB behind. CH's first duty is to prevent him from entering the circle. Yet CH needs cover in case he is beaten. As RB moves to give this cover he will have to have

an eye open for the possible OR to CF pass. Similarly, RH has to watch IL. OL is the forward left open. He is the least dangerous and should a pass be made to him, RH would hope to

A free back system is designed to allow for the possibility of an extra attacker coming through: hence the movement of S (or a CB if a pair were being used). See the diagram above. There is no point at all in LWB staying out on his man in this situation, a consideration which may be overlooked if rigid man-to-man marking has been ordained.
The maxim always is: *guard against the greatest danger.*

Depth

Without depth the whole defence will be penetrated by one through pass. When four-back systems employing two in the centre first came into English hockey, one of the outstanding tactical deficiencies was the tendency in some teams for them to play in a line approximately parallel to the goal line. This resulted in the hapless goalkeeper being left uncovered to face a forward running unchallenged onto a through pass.

Cross-passing by attackers may result in defenders losing depth as they re-orientate to the new threat. If it occurs, attackers hope to seize the moment to pass the ball through them.

Depth permits cover. Preferably it should be based on the triangles, but even with only two players, cover means that, should the first be beaten, the second still bars the attacker's way. Cover provided by depth is not only of team-mates but also of space.

Support

As in attack tactics, support interlocks with depth. When a defender is faced by an opponent, his decision to tackle may be influenced by the presence or absence of a supporter. Until support comes up he may feel his best plan is to police or delay his opponent. The supporter should so position himself that if his partner's tackle is unsuccessful and he is beaten, he himself can make a follow-up tackle before the opponent regains full control of the ball. It will often be advantageous for the supporter to tell his partner when he is in position.

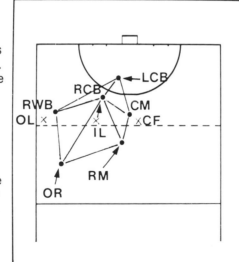

Triangles of support for RCB facing IL
LCB has moved to support from behind (cover) and OR and RM to support from in front by opening angles for quick passes

If the tackle is successful, the defender will frequently need to make a quick pass. His nearby team-mates will be able to help if they are thinking in terms of triangles; more distant ones should be striving for spaces where they may receive safely and without the pass being intercepted.

Delay – Non-committal

Mention has already been made of the need to hold up advancing attackers until a tackle may safely be made.

The diagram on p. 92 is taken from play. It affords a gross example of a breach of the principle of delay where a double mistake by RWB turned a favourable 3 v. 2 situation on his side of the field into disaster. He not only left his own man open, but charged in to tackle a player some distance away, who at that stage was threatening no danger to the intact defence. This rash and headlong attempt was easily evaded, IL passing through to OL, who, having drawn the CBs over, was able to centre across the head of the circle. Quite correctly OR had raced into the IR position. He met the pass and scored. (It is also worth observing that the LWB for some reason never appeared in the picture!) Had RWB been content to bide his time by moving to ensure that

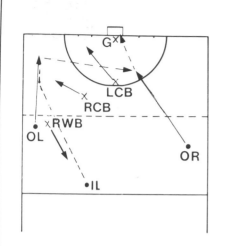

IL could not find OL, this debacle would have been avoided.

It should be noted that when a team loses possession well upfield, the first step to delay the counter-attack, and so win time for players to deploy defensively, should be taken by the advanced elements. So many forwards need to be schooled into defensive reactions as soon as possession goes. In this situation, depending on their relation to the ball, they should either be harrying to regain possession, so putting pressure on the opponent, or moving to intercept forward passes. If their opponents can only play the ball square, this in itself gains precious seconds for the defence. Midfields can exert a similar influence, again depending on the exact tactical position, by marking either opponents or space valuable to them.

For the individual player, delay and non-committal may require psychological restraint especially if faced by a cunning and able opponent seeking to draw him out from the defensive network. In the diagram on the left, RWB exhibited a signal lack of restraint!

Coaching the Principles and Systems

Paradoxically, the first thing with youngsters and novices is to forget the systems. They will eventually follow on naturally when the principles have become sufficiently well understood. Ensure the players have sufficient space in which to achieve success without *undue* difficulty and keep numbers down at the start to give plenty of ball contact. **The aim is to inculcate understanding.** Adopt a simple approach and be patient.

In Attack

There are two aspects of this: individual skill and team play. Too much restriction will inhibit individual skill, which, as already urged, should be encouraged, as in taking on defenders and shooting. In some practices, therefore, conditions may be applied to this end—e.g. the player must beat his immediate opponent before passing within a certain range of goal (say within the third square of an area three grids long), or must shoot in the circle.

Yet the demands of team play cannot be overlooked. Self-expression becomes excessive when the player begins to put himself before his team. Then he must be stopped. To emphasise the team aspect such conditions as one-two (two touch) hockey—i.e. 'one' to receive, 'two' to pass, no running with the ball, and no tackling by opponent—may be applied.

Simple exercises in grids or other suitable areas can bring out such elementary matters as
- Support—not only from behind, but also to offer passing angles
- Establishing width.

Many club players will exhibit a marked lack of mobility and imagination.

In Defence

Organisation and the *understanding* of that organisation are necessary to safeguard the goal and to regain possession. Organisation will break down without individual and team discipline. Some of the following exercises seek to instil organisation and discipline in the face of lost possession and attack by opponents.

A very useful aid in instilling discipline is to decide on a pattern of play appropriate to the size of the team. Thus four might play to an inverted Y

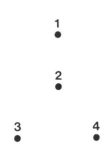

1 •
2 •
3 • 4 •

and six as a pyramid.

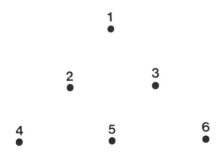

1 •
2 • 3 •
4 • 5 • 6 •

Incidentally the first of these could relate easily to a CB and three midfields and the second to three midfields and three forwards, or CH and five forwards.

When possession is lost, the team must re-form in its selected pattern goal-side of the attackers. This type of movement also paves the way for understanding zonal defensive systems. This theme may be developed to combine man-to-man and zonal marking.

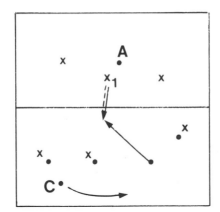

As the X players cross into their opponents' half they are picked up man-for-man.

C has moved to cover and A must hurry into a goalside position of X1

Appreciation of the basic principles can and should begin at quite an early stage. For instance, in the grid practices as soon as a team consists of three players work can start on the concept of operational triangles. When a fourth is added, considerations of indirect involvement outside the immediate triangle arise, e.g.:

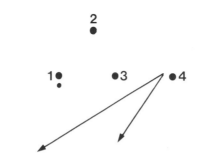

4, being out of 1's immediate triangle, has to think where he will be the most use to his little team. Some possibilities are shown

Any of many variable factors could apply. Suppose that 2 were already bursting forward. Then 4 might well consider his best move would be to restore depth and support from behind.

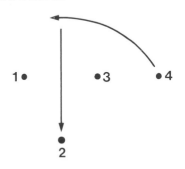

In both attack and defence the aim is to stimulate the whole team —however many players— to appreciate that every man has his part to play in that particular phase of the game. As numbers grow involvement becomes more complex, hence the necessity for patience on the part of the coach. If numbers are added gradually and the principles driven home and fully understood at each stage, when the eleven-a-side is reached players will be much more able to adapt, *whatever the system*.

Tactical Topics

The Extra Man

A shot at goal means that an attacker has not been effectively marked, albeit perhaps only momentarily. Briefly, therefore, he was the extra man. This extra man may be obtained in various ways, including the following:

● **Stickwork.** E.g. the attacker takes on and beats the last defender out of goal. Often this will be the only way against an intact defence.
In another context it may amount to drawing an opponent to open the way for a pass. The value of the shut-out (see p. 34) is emphasised.

● **Rapid passing.** A succession of first-time, or nearly so, passes made with precision can also open a defence but calls for a very high level of skill.

● **Coming from behind.** This is dealt with additionally in other sections. Adding players from deeper positions is a powerful weapon for obtaining numerical superiority. Alternatively, the extra man, instead of going through himself, may act as a staging post for a telling pass. He must have space in which to operate. If it does not exist his team-mates in front must open it for him.

Examples using the RWB are:

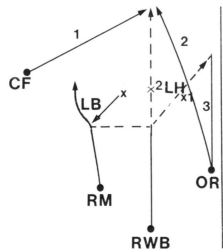

Another move, shown as for LWB, is:

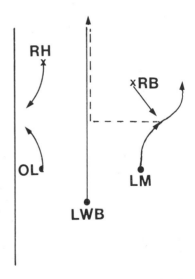

RWB acting as staging post for pass for either CF (1) or OR (2) to collect with LH at 1. Pass to OR (3) is used with LH at 2 to cut off (1) and (2)

England forward Verona Nolan shooting for the North against the West. Note the well-controlled follow-through

Montreal, 1976. New Zealand defending against Belgium

off his marker to collect and shoot.

He will he helped in this if his opponent concentrates too intently on the ball (ball watching). With X firmly focusing on the ball,

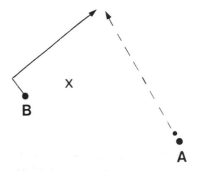

with A, B, whom he is supposed to be marking, may be able to drift away unnoticed then turn to collect A's through pass. B's movement is generally said to be 'blind side' of X, i.e. where X cannot see him. X in fact is guilty of grave error in not adjusting his own position to keep B in sight.

When several players are able to move about in front of and amongst defenders there is a good chance, assuming that the running is purposeful and understood by team-mates, that a harassed defence will grow anxious and confused, allowing an attacker to receive safely in space.

In both diagrams space for WB has been made by the wings going wide and by midfields taking the backs infield by threatening to beat them on the inside. Timing and accuracy of passing are required to enable the WB to accelerate on to the ball and move it forward without checking.

The following diagram shows the commonest runs by midfields (here four are assumed) overlapping their forwards. The natural run by outside midfields is between CF and the wing. Coaches will often find that both the midfield and wing concerned need to be alerted to and practised in outside overlaps by the midfield.

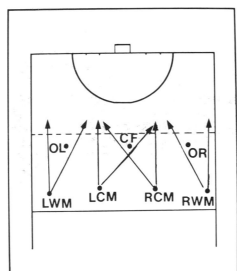

Diagrammatic representation of the commoner runs of 4 midfields ahead of a 3-forward formation

● **Player's own movement.** By such tricks as explosive starts from a standstill, unexpected acceleration and doubling back, a player may be able to throw

Scissors movements with or without transference of the ball may achieve the same result, perhaps by opening space for a forward dash by a deeper player. One possibility is:

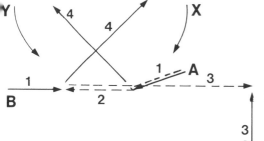

A, with ball, and B approach each other (1) drawing their markers, X and Y, with them. Taking care not to obstruct, A passes to B (2), who squares the ball out for C to run on to (3) through the space opened by X. A and B veer away (4), quite possibly confusing X and Y unless they are well trained. A variation involving a reverse pass (see p. 52) is:

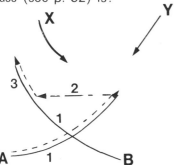

A draws X and attracts Y by looking as if he may attack him while B runs behind A(1). A then passes to B(2) to receive and take on (3) through the space.

Specimen Place-Changing Exercises

1. In pairs – Scissors
A starts with the ball and runs with it diagonally to A¹, ahead of B, who crosses over behind him to B¹ to receive the pass. B repeats. For reverse-stick passing B starts. Accuracy and sufficient length in the pass are vital. Add opposition, passive or active, as required.

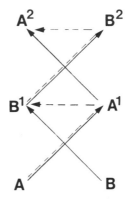

2. In threes – Coming from Behind
A and B start level, but C is ahead of B, who has the ball and passes it to him. A advances to A¹ for the square pass from C, B

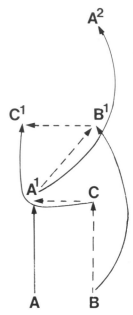

meanwhile running ahead of C to B¹. C, having passed, runs behind A to position ahead of him at C¹. A passes to B¹, running ahead to A², B¹ meanwhile passing square to C¹. Begin by walking through this exercise.

For reverse-stick practice ball starts with A who has C in front of him.

Although these and similar exercises should be practised by all out-players – and improvised goals may be set up for shots for the goalkeeper to save at the end of one run – they must especially be practised by players likely to be combining together, e.g. Exercise 1 by inner and wing. These functional groups should study the various problems which will arise. Players introduced as opposition will be able to assist in this.

It is important to ensure that square passes are square, and *not* diagonal, to avoid interception.

The Hook

This is a particular, much neglected and very important tactic in the attack. Wings are most usually involved, but all out-players should be aware of what is required.

Wings have a wide variety of centres at their disposal. The one which should only be used when a definite opening clearly exists is the square centre about half-way up the circle. Nearly always it travels into a ruck of players. There will be other occasions when no useful inwards pass is open. The hook, as I call it, may then be used; it is also valuable as a surprise variation to the centre.

The wing hooks in making for a position near the goal-line and just inside the circle. *Any man in possession behind them is a danger to defenders.* The hook achieves this situation and has the additional bonus that if the wing has broken away, his supporting players need to cover less ground to reach effective supporting positions.

Whether playing from right or left the supporting players must aim to provide the wing with the maximum number of passes. These radiate from him rather as

fingers from the palm of the hand. From the right, a most important position is the one where a traditional IR would expect to operate, though it could equally be the RH (RWB) who finds himself there. *Somebody must,* however, be there. Two possible deployments are shown, each offering four passing possibilities:

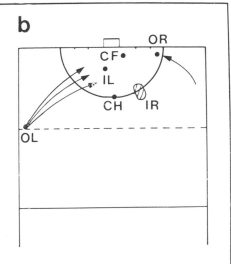

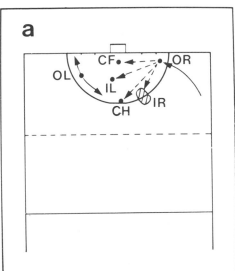

The principal differences concern the CF and OL. In diagram **a** the CF is centrally placed and can move towards the pass. The other view is that as in diagram **b** he would be slightly ball side of the nearer post. In both diagrams OL has the task of collecting the ball,

as from deflections, should it travel across the circle that far. Diagram **b** shows the ideal method where he starts late and moves in at speed, so throwing off anyone marking him. This is more difficult than the action required from him in diagram **a**, where he is already in the circle. IR has been given a shaded area in both diagrams. Again, ideally he comes in onto the ball for a snap shot, but the main thing is to ensure that a man is in that area near the circle line.

The greatest cause of failure is over-eagerness on the part of the five supporting players, especially the four nearest to the ball. If, as so frequently occurs, they all rush towards the goal, OR loses his passing opportunities. It is essential that they remain spaced over the depth of the circle with CH and IR very near the edge. The closer in they go, the more easily are they marked.

In principle these factors also apply on the left, with the IR taking over the same position relatively as IL. Modifications occur because of the extra difficulty of pulling the ball back from the left side. This especially affects the IL, who will expect a reverse-stick pass. As this may be made square, i.e. at right-angles from the goal-line, or even backwards of square, the IL must position himself accordingly. To ensure a first-time shot being available for IL, OL needs to go farther into the circle than OR. Other considerations affecting forwards on the goal-line are covered in Scoring Goals, p. 57.

Marking and Cover

There are two basic methods of marking, man-to-man and zonal. What happens in most games is that players adapt to using either one or the other as appropriate. Neither provides all the answers to the problems which mobile intelligent attackers may pose.

Man-to-Man

At international level this reached its peak of popularity arising from

Montreal, 1976. Where would the West German No. 11, attacking the Spanish goal, have liked support? Note the umpire's excellent position

the West German men's team use of it around 1972. When possession is lost each player is required to pick up his personal opponent and mark him closely right up until possession is regained. It calls for such outstanding fitness and individual and team discipline as to make it impractical for any but highly trained sides. It fails when an opponent dislodges his marker from the defensive network by beating him or by escaping to receive a pass in space. Against a rigid man-to-man system, if two attackers move towards each other a space *must* be opened. Ideally defenders will hope to have a covering player who deals with the man who receives the ball in that space; hence the use of a sweeper.

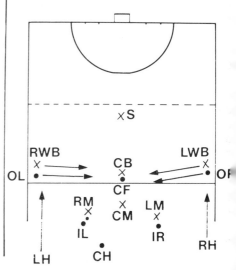

Man-to-man marking conceding space
By running towards CF, ostensibly looking for a pass and taking their markers with them, the wings open space on the flanks.

If LH receives the pass, having drawn S, he could cross-pass to RH running through

Marking in this method requires a player to be so close to his opponent that he is able to tackle immediately his man receives the ball. If his opponent is not about to receive he is still within a yard of him.

Zonal Marking

In this defenders assume responsibility for opponents entering their own particular area of the pitch, the size and shape of which will be determined by the given tactical situation. Thus teams attacking on a broad front force defenders into accepting wider-spread areas with the real chance that they will not be able to cover all the ground. If in a 4–3–3 system all seven backs and midfields, or, in the 2–3–2–3, the seven backs, halves and insides, achieve positions goal-side of the attackers, the defence is very strong. If they do not, gaps may appear. With either system the wings and CF may be tackling back and harrying.

Attackers will naturally try to draw defenders from their zones and to move from one zone to another. If one defender is drawn out, another takes his place; and if two attackers enter one zone another defender does so too.

Combined

Sometimes a team elects to man-to-man mark a particularly dangerous opponent, the most usual being the CF. On occasion it may be still more profitable to mark out the devastating passer. For the rest, the defence adopts the zonal method.

During a game a team is most likely to go over temporarily to a man-to-man basis when facing free hits inside their own Defence Area. Every single attacker must then be marked very tightly. In the middle the goalkeeper will advance to limit space for any through pass and to that extent, and if the only man available, in effect becomes the cover there. It is also quite common for teams using four backs to close mark the wings and CF when faced by a developing attack. The sweeper or one of the centre backs provides the cover.

Marking versus Cover

When defenders are able to mark all the immediate attackers and still maintain cover, no conflict arises. Yet attackers will always be striving to attain numerical superiority or at least parity. When they succeed in this, defenders will speedily have to evaluate the twin and rival claims of cover and marking.

This type of problem has been discussed under Concentration, p. 89, but defenders must fully realise that their first priority is the immediate or most dangerous threat. Here is another example to drive home the point.

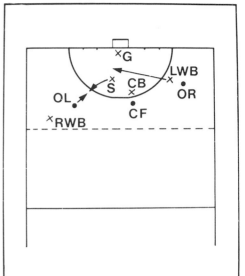

Cover before marking

The threat is on the defenders' right. If OL beats S he will be in for an unchallenged shot. LWB must cover to try to prevent this. Although CB may try to withdraw slightly he cannot move so far from CF as to give him the chance of a shot off a pass from OL.

In the circle there is no choice between cover and marking if an opponent is free with the chance of receiving the ball to shoot. There may still be no choice in certain circumstances outside the circle either.

Additional Notes on Playing Positions

The goalkeeper is dealt with on pp. 109–118.

These notes supplement what has been written elsewhere on the play of the three divisions of out-players. Their numbers vary. These comments are therefore general rather than specific.

The aim of teachers and coaches should be primarily to develop highly competent, versatile hockey players before they become channelled into some form of specialisation. I have said this before and do so again because England managers of the men's team have been urging it for many years without producing the desired effect.

Basic ability is assumed throughout these notes but some positions do call for emphasised attributes. As I have also said before, even players of great all-round ability will have qualities suiting them particularly well for certain positions.

Backs

Skills

The predominantly needed skills are the ability to win the ball and to clear with power, speed and accuracy. Therefore, backs must master all forms of tackling (see pp. 44–52) and be expert purposeful hitters of the ball, not mere unthinking clouters. So many players, not just backs, burden their team with unnecessary work by delivering passes to their opponents. Whenever possible, exercises and practices for backs – as after making a tackle – should include giving a useful pass, possibly followed by supporting movement off the ball. A strong reverse-side tackle is of special value to left side defenders.

Backs, especially CBs, must be good markers.

In Defence

Apart from marking their individual opponents and generally maintaining the security of their team, backs will try to deny the circle to their opponents, with, wherever possible, the main defensive stand being made on the *edge* of the Defence Area (see p. 11). Teams playing 2-back systems need the help of WHs (or WMs) by taking the WFs.

The centre of the field must be the most dangerous area. Hence the systems which deploy two backs to guard it. Sometimes a third back – e.g. making two CBs and a free back – can be given for greater protection still.

On the other hand a team may adopt a defensive strategy based on using only one central rear defender. In defensive phases the centre midfield(s) carry the heavy responsibility of judging when to join the backs.

In Attack

Backs who cannot attack cannot play their full part in a normally integrated team effort. When they go forward they must have the knowledge that any potential danger behind them will be covered. They cannot attack strongly if psychologically they are looking over their shoulder. Customarily the RWB will go forward most. Here flair for breaking out will often make the difference between a competent and a very good player. The player with the right temperament, will automatically be looking for any chance to go forward and will automatically seize it at once. The following diagrams illustrate two possibilities:

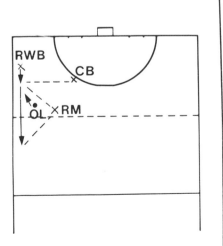

RWB runs onto the 16-yds hit from CB. He goes forward, evading OL by means of a one-two (wall pass) with RM. If the opposing LM intervenes, RM will be open for a return pass; if he does not, the opposing LWB will be confronted by both RWB and OR.

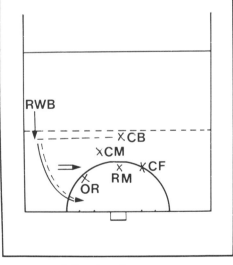

⇒ =general direction of movements to open space

A rehearsed free hit. Space has been opened for RWB, again coming onto the pass from behind, by the movement of OR, RM and CF to their left and by CM moving in advance of CB to make space for the pass behind him.

The Sweeper

Any back or midfield may find himself acting as a sweeper. His duties, which are not always fully appreciated, are:

● **Cover**
  Behind the backs by moving laterally. His movements exemplify the practical value of the theory of players operating in triangles.

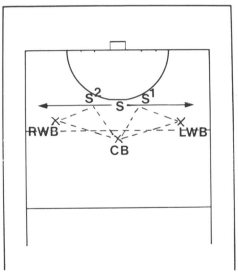

The sweeper's covering, at S^1 to form the triangle with LWB and CB against a right side attack and at S^2 with RWB and CB against a left side attack

Other members of the triangles will be midfields on occasion.

Marking

Unlike his fellow backs in front of him, he has no specific opponent to mark. This is the whole point of the 'free back' systems. He is responsible for any attacker coming through.

Sweeping-up through passes

These will often be hotly pursued, emphasising the need for quick, forceful and accurate hitting. Security must predominate. Frequently there will be no option but to find touch. Nevertheless the sweeper should be looking to make a constructive clearance, especially to target men upfield, whenever safe. As a general indication, except when replacing another back (see next point), the sweeper will confine himself to about the middle 40 yds of the pitch. Attempts will be made to draw him out to a flank. He should not, however, go very wide unless he can do so in complete security — as he often can with long through passes.

Replacing another back

When appropriate the sweeper will take over this position when another back goes forward. Should he himself be able to take what will in all probability be only the vary rare chance to go forward, he must be covered very quickly.

Calling

With all the play in front of him the sweeper is best placed to give general advice and to call the marking to his backs. This is a vital skill, especially when opponents are adding men from behind or are place-changing across the defence.

With rigid man-to-man marking the backs will closely follow their individual opponents, who will assuredly seek to lure them into false positions to create gaps for other opponents coming from behind. Typically the CF will move out wide.

If the man-to-man marking is not being rigidly applied, the CB would not move too far with him. Fine judgement may be needed to decide just how far the CB does go before passing on the CF to another defender. The usual factors will influence not only the moment of handing over but also to whom it is made.

Should the sweeper be too heavily committed, someone else — e.g. the goalkeeper — must be prepared and able to undertake the calling.

Centre Backs

As the CBs are concerned either with the CF in 3-forward systems or with twin CFs in 4-forward systems and not with the inners (midfields), their switching to afford cover to each other is much shallower than when playing in their traditional ACH system roles. As play approaches the goal, the switching becomes still shallower or may not occur at all. This is to prevent an opponent being able to lie up too close to goal, to avoid unsighting the goalkeeper and because of insufficient time to switch before a shot is made. Depth and cover are essential in defence. The backs may ensure this by one or both of two means, the covering back and the diagonal line as used by traditional halves. It is the lack of cover behind the single centre back with no sweeper which leads some to believe that three backs are insufficient to deal with swift, skilful forwards.

Midfields
Requirements

A case can be made for claiming that any one element of a team is the most important. There is no doubt that the hardest working are the midfields. They have to be good defenders as well as good forwards. Fitness must be of a high order for their skill levels to be sustained in spite of all their running and other activity.

More than anyone else they are involved in changes of role, from defence to attack and vice versa. Adept reading of play is essential.

Ideally midfields should be interchangeable.

In Attack

IFs, the predecessors of midfields, have always been looked upon as schemers. To turn this to advantage midfields must be able to pass precisely. In addition they must themselves want to go forward and especially want to score.

They may have more scoring opportunities by coming from behind than forwards in advanced positions who are already closely marked.

How and where a midfield becomes in effect a forward depends on the usual tactical factors. In case of conflict between them the player has to depend on his experience and tactical sense to give him the correct answers. Often, however, there will be no conflict.

OL has the ball. Supporting by moving towards the ball is often a useful rule of thumb. Here is a chance for 2 v. 1 on RH.

LM notes further that OL is going as wide as possible and that CF has moved right. He also sees that RH and CH have conformed, leaving space for him. All these factors point to his moving up for a square, or slightly behind square pass which will give him time to

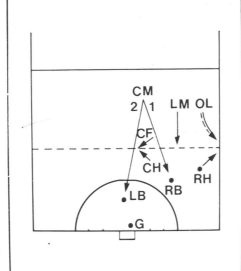

receive and control before RB can attack.

Developing this a stage further, a far-sighted CM might support in front and might

- attack RB (Run 1) to give LM a 2 v. 1 there
- having faith in his LM and OL to defeat their men, plan still further ahead and engage the covering LB (Run 2).

Note that with either run he becomes a new CF.

In Defence

Good defensive play, even more than good attacking play, depends on the sound triangles formed by the players concerned. Upfield distances may be considerable, but as opposing attacks develop the triangles become closer-knit. In the early stages of meeting an attack, a midfield will often be the apex of his triangle, for instance:

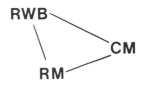

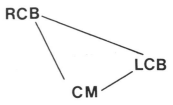

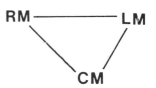

Preferably he will tackle early as his opponent prepares to receive or whilst he is trying to control the ball. He should aim to keep the attackers from playing the ball forward so that other defenders

have time to move to covering positions. In other circumstances, he may be able to tempt an attacker to pass across an area when he knows he can intercept. Nevertheless, the maxim is not to go for an interception which, if missed, will put the defender out of the game.
One of the most difficult problems for a midfield is to achieve a balance between his two roles. Although the theory is simple, its practical application may not be. When his side are attacking he is free to support where and how appropriate; when they are defending his position is between his immediate adversary and goal.

O RM (off diagram) has been supporting an attack which has failed. It is physically impossible for him to move to his normal defensive position goal-side of X IL. This highlights two points:

■ The need for defensive balance behind RM so that someone can move on to his free opponent. In a team playing with a marking-free midfield, here CM, this would be his task.

■ The need in the X team for the IL (or LM) to be a skilled attacker able to capitalise on his freedom from RM.

Forwards

It is generally considered that defence play is easier because in general terms

● The ball tends to approach defenders from their front, whilst forwards often receive from behind.

● Defence depends on organisation; attack on flair and initiative.

● Scoring goals (see pp. 57–61) needs a higher degree of accuracy than much defence work.

● In comparison, forwards have

Shooting under pressure. (Dorrie Sadler's Dutch opponent has needlessly reduced her reach in this poor tackling position)

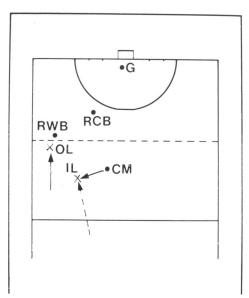

to perform more of their skills when moving at speed.

Perhaps, therefore, more than anybody, the expert and goal-scoring forward needs the capacity for infinite practising. Highly proficient stick-work must rank amongst the top priorities of a forward. Training in this cannot start too soon for the youngster, who must be prepared to undertake much practice on his own.

Forwards above all must have the courage to risk failure when they shoot. Especially in the men's game, undeterred by knocks, they must also have the courage — bred of confidence — to use their skill to the full. This will mean engaging defenders. The greater their repertoire for beating an opponent (see p. 33), the greater the chances of a successful outcome. This in turn may at least establish a moral superiority, even if not providing the immediate chance of a shot at goal.

Despite the heavy stress on shooting in this book, there will be many occasions in which the path to goal is blocked. Forwards should then be prepared to attack wide, very wide. The middle third or half of the pitch is often so congested as to give no scope for manoeuvre. Turning a flank is a secondary target.

Having gone wide, the forward should generally be aiming to establish the situation described in the Hook, p. 99. His team-mates must recognise what is happening and seek their correct supporting positions.

Combined play has been dealt with elsewhere, but players cannot fully exploit their flair and initiative without being alert to the many rapid tactical changes as they occur. To do this they need to scan, as brought out under Dribbling, p. 21. Most players do not move their heads sufficiently to pick up the movements of both their own and opposing men. Many very rapid decisions have to be made in attacking play. The wider the player's grasp of the tactical situation, the more likely he is to make correct ones. Whether, and if so how, or not to attack a defender provides an example. Whilst there is no intention of gainsaying what has been written under Beating an Opponent (see p. 33), an analysis of the situation shows that many factors obtain. For instance:

■ An opponent is not beaten until the ball is past him. This does not necessarily mean engaging him at close quarters, however.

■ The distance of an attacker from defender and defender from his circle. If it is truly a 1 v. 1 situation the defender will try to delay committal until he can rely on his goalkeeper's support. The attacker must try to engage him before that moment.

■ Other potential support for the defender. The attacker must decide whether or not he has time to attack his man before support can arrive. If the attacker, previous to receiving the ball, has concentrated solely on his colleague passing to him, he may well be ignorant of the position of potential supporters.

■ Support for the attacker. Awareness of the position of team-mates may clearly indicate that the correct course is for the attacker merely to draw the defender and then pass.

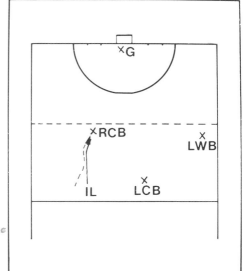

IL must engage at once — before help arrives for RCB and to prevent him retreating to gain support from G

It is in these circumstances that the forward will need his full repertoire and his best tricks. It is unwise to show everything too early in the match.

Offside

It is quite true that often the penalised forward was not responsible for being offside. Forwards may be pushed up offside by players behind them delaying their passes too long. Nevertheless, forwards are caught offside through carelessness. This particularly applies to wings, who can take in the whole width of the pitch at a glance.

One safe method of avoiding offside in an attack is to stay behind the ball until it is played ahead. This simple method could be used far more. A little thought and restraint are all that is needed.

Remember: offside may mean the missed chance of a shot.

Special points to remember:

- **Determination** – to be first for the ball. Follow up any shot at goal and go for the half-chance.
- **Collection.** When possible, having collected change course.
- **Co-operation.** Be aware of

A stupid offside
IR has carefully kept behind the ball; OL, by his foolish run, has ruined a fine goal-scoring chance

By staying slightly behind, Verona Nolan has remained on-side for the short pass from Denise Parry, and has an open goal for England

players coming through. Help them by making space. Co-operate with other players in tactical running. At present this receives little attention.
- **Defensive tasks.** As circumstances demand: tackle back, harass or pursue your man. Move goal-side of the ball unless it is too far back in your own half, or, more particularly, interdict probable passes. Support a colleague likely to want to pass.

In an integrated team, forwards are as much defenders when possession is lost as backs are attackers when possession is gained.

The Goalkeeper

Goalkeeping requires specialised skills. It also calls for an outlook rather different from other players'.

This is not to say that, as some think, a goalkeeper is slightly mad. This concept probably arises from the fact that the successful goalkeeper may be less alive than others to the potential danger of facing a hard-hit ball. A goalkeeper has from time to time to accept hard blows from the ball on places other than the pads. Perhaps the most important characteristic of the aspiring goalkeeper is reliability. The unreliable goalkeeper, despite occasional no doubt spectacular saves, may well upset the morale of his side.

Good goalkeepers naturally do bring off the spectacular, but basically they manage to make many things look deceptively simple. This depends on being in the right place at the right moment, which cannot be achieved without anticipation and quick decisions. Here experience, as from match play and functional practices, is indispensable. Whatever his mental prowess in these respects, however, the goalkeeper must also have the necessary physical attributes of fast reaction, speed and agility. Yet reliability has deeper foundations such as a justifiable, but not over-weening, confidence, a refusal to be put off by any bad luck, and a cool acceptance of responsibility. Perhaps these foundations can be summed up as temperament.

The goalkeeper does bear the peculiar responsibility of being the one who, more than anybody else, can lose the match by a single mistake. Conversely, there is the satisfaction of an 'on' day, when, however hard the opponents try, inspired goalkeeping wins the match.

Kicking

This to a spectator is the most obvious of the goalkeeper's special skills. For the first time for the men, the 1975 Rules contained a clause (Rule 12, I(d)) specifically forbidding dangerous kicking. It highlights a traditional fundamental difference in approach between women and men. Men have always admired the high soaring kick pitching half-way up the field; women have always tended to penalise any lofted kicking.

Perhaps in the past men's umpires have been inclined to be over-lenient. Contrariwise, to condemn such kicks automatically is as unjustified as automatically penalising other forms of aerial play.

Boys begin with an advantage over girls since they kick naturally with a strong back-swing. The basic female kick is made with the inside of the foot or big toe, whilst men favour the instep or

toes. Advocates of the women's push-kick, however, consider it more accurate.

Technique

A goalkeeper should go for:

- **Security,** as he must in all his play, except in desperation. If the whole width of the pad can be presented, as in kicking along the line of the ball, there is much more scope for dealing with the ball which 'moves' off the pitch. Awkwardly bouncing, often mis-hit, balls need special care, for they are so easily mis-kicked. If in any doubt, the goalkeeper should stop the ball before clearing.
- **Power:** Back-swing, forceful follow-through and timing are the ingredients, plus, as in hitting, the forward movement of body weight in running into the kick.

- **Accuracy:** Ideally the goalkeeper will try to direct his kick to retain possession, or, when this is not possible, safely into touch to relieve pressure. What he must avoid is interception by an opponent.

Most parts of the foot may be used and if the ball is hit below centre it will rise. For this to happen with the modern Continental type kicker, which has a large rhomboid type toe, the ball must be approaching several inches off the ground. With other types a slight ground unevenness will often allow the foot to strike below centre. For the long instep or toe kick the supporting foot comes down close to the ball with the kicking foot hitting it at the bottom of its swing and the powerful follow-through continuing along the line of flight. The encumbrance of pads and

kickers prevents many of the refinements of soccer players, though some rotation of the hips, as in screw kicking when the line of the ball is deliberately altered through many degrees, is sometimes possible. The head should be over the ball.

The inner side of the foot is used by men for sweeping square away from oncoming forwards or for short passing, while the outer side is mainly used as an emergency measure or for a very short pass. All goalkeepers must be proficient with *both* feet.

Saving

The first thing with novices is to eradicate any tendency to try to stop with the stick any shot which can be conveniently saved by something else. The stick is for emergency saves: first priority is pads and kickers and second priority body and hands. Whenever possible, the goalkeeper should be standing ready for the shot, having completed any necessary forward movement, and not still be moving towards it when it comes.

Pads and Kickers

In saving with the pads, generally the goalkeeper needs to be certain of keeping the ball within his control, though occasionally he will have to play for a lengthy rebound to put the ball through

Another England goalkeeper, Hazel Feltwell, clearing for the Midlands against the West with a lunge-kick

Cushioning a shot

on-rushing forwards. To keep control the ball must be cushioned by a slight give of the legs on impact or by bringing the knees a little downwards and forwards. The stance needs to be poised, weight slightly forward, and body relaxed. An all-too-common error, particularly reprehensible at penalty corners, is for the goalkeeper to fall backwards when saving. This is entirely due to the weight being backwards instead of as recommended. Control with the older type pads is easier than with the Continental.

It has to be accepted that if the ball strikes the kicker, the goalkeeper will have very little if any influence over the rebound.

To avoid having the ball jam between the feet, some authorities believe in placing the back of one heel against the other instep. It is then possible to move the ball with the front foot.

Shots to the side present more of a problem. The farther away they are, the more they test the goalkeeper's agility. For shots on or near to the ground, he should try to offer the full width of the pad to combat any unexpected movement of the ball. This is achieved by having the side of the heel grounded.

With shots far to the side it will be all the goalkeeper can do to save them. For the nearer ones he should, however, try to preserve his balance so that he can clear immediately with foot or stick.

Hands and Body

Let the ball come on to them.
Although Rule 12, II(d) allows for rebounds from the goalkeeper denied to other players, striking at the ball with the hand, such movements as palming over the bar and breasting the ball are all illegal and in many instances will be penalised by a penalty stroke. Even when diving to save, try to avoid striking the ball.

Only the hand and *not* the stick must be used for the ball above the shoulder.

Stick

The stick can be a valuable last line of defence when nothing more substantial can be put in the path of the ball. This is especially so when saving at full length by the right post. The stick may also be the only means of intercepting a pass a few yards out across the face of goal.

Clearances

These fall into two main categories: those made from a freely running ball and those made following a save. In the first, the goalkeeper will rely nearly always upon kicking. Exceptions would be when compelled to play the ball outside the circle and when the ball can be reached only with the stick.

The speedy, mobile and powerful kicker is likely to dominate his circle and to establish a moral advantage over his opponents. He will also forcibly demonstrate his value in initiating counter-attacks. The stick tends to come into its own more after a save and at other close-quarters work. Often it will be used in an unorthodox way, as when the goalkeeper is prone, and sometimes for a one-handed sweep. Goalkeepers ought therefore to be skilled in stick techniques, not forgetting the value of the scoop for playing a

dead ball, particularly on a muddy surface.

When the hand has been used to a high ball, the stick may be used to play it as it lands, though more frequently the goalkeeper will prefer to kick it on the volley or half-volley as less time is needed. He should be trained to clear the ball as swiftly as possible – which sometimes will mean diving to do so – after any save. If on occasion there is less urgency, that should be regarded as a bonus and one to be used constructively.

The golden rule when clearing is to make the clearance wide and flat, though when given that bonus a counter-attacking pass should be made if it is *certainly* safe from interception (see Security, p. 89).

Positioning

Primarily this is based on 'narrowing the angle', the method by which a goalkeeper offers to his opponent the smallest possible target.

The diagram illustrates how this is accomplished. P, Q and R are opponents at various positions and G1 is the goalkeeper on his line in the middle of his goal. In this position he has done nothing to reduce the size of the target. Suppose, however, he were at G2 for a shot from P. A comparison of the line through G2 with the width of the goal through G1 shows how the target has been

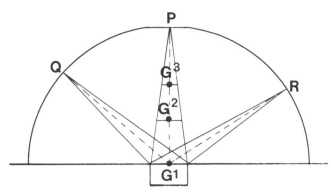

intersection of PG1 at about 2 yds from goal. The arc is a guide. If, for example, P were shooting, the goalkeeper would try to reach a position farther from his line, though with other forwards in the circle he would need to be aware of the possibility of a lateral pass. When the goalkeeper faces an attacker at a very flat angle, above all, he must ensure that the shot does not squeeze between him and the post. He will, therefore, move hard up to the post with his pad slightly overlapping. He will hope to save shots aimed inside the other post

reduced by narrowing the angle. The target is still smaller with the goalkeeper at G3. Similar considerations apply by movements from G1 along the dotted lines towards Q and R. How far towards an opponent about to shoot a goalkeeper may or should advance is complicated by various other factors such as

the time available and the disposition of other players.
If, however, he is near his goal and faced with an immediate shot coming at medium to long range, he must move a little way towards his opponent. For shots from different points he tends to move on an arc. This runs from post to post and passes through the

Forcing a shot wide

Stick clearance — under pressure!

by extending his 'outside' leg, stick or hand. He will leave his post to tackle the opponent closing in only if *sure* of winning the ball or as a last resort.

The danger, and a very real one, is the pass across goal. Thoughtful attackers in favourable circumstances will play it so that he cannot intercept. If, however, it is inaccurately played but still outside the reach of his foot, the goalkeeper can dive away from his post — possibly using that for his push-off — at right angles to the line to intercept with stick or hand.

Goalkeepers need a sixth sense of knowing where their goal is behind them without looking. Formerly they used a variety of marks scraped on the ground with the stick to help, but nowadays this is forbidden by Rule 4 (g). The special positionings at penalty strokes, penalty corners and corners is dealt with under their respective sections (see pp. 139, 132 and 137).

Tackling

Determination is even more important to the goalkeeper than to anyone else. *No one* must be allowed to hinder his effort to rob the opponent in possession. The goalkeeper can help his friends by calling 'Mine' clearly. They must get out of his way without question or hesitation — or take the consequences! Timing is of comparable importance. It will decide both how and when to strike for the ball.

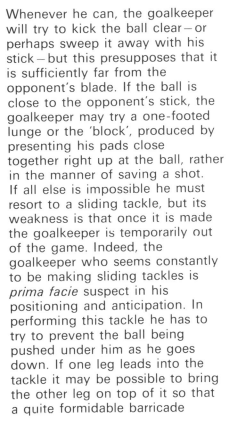

Whenever he can, the goalkeeper will try to kick the ball clear – or perhaps sweep it away with his stick – but this presupposes that it is sufficiently far from the opponent's blade. If the ball is close to the opponent's stick, the goalkeeper may try a one-footed lunge or the 'block', produced by presenting his pads close together right up at the ball, rather in the manner of saving a shot. If all else is impossible he must resort to a sliding tackle, but its weakness is that once it is made the goalkeeper is temporarily out of the game. Indeed, the goalkeeper who seems constantly to be making sliding tackles is *prima facie* suspect in his positioning and anticipation. In performing this tackle he has to try to prevent the ball being pushed under him as he goes down. If one leg leads into the tackle it may be possible to bring the other leg on top of it so that a quite formidable barricade confronts the opponent.

Some goalkeepers are prone to tackle wide too far out – covered under Positioning – and to tackle prematurely. It is nearly always a mistake to go in when a team-mate has a fair chance of taking the ball or when a mêlée has developed. The answer is to hover, poised within striking range, to pounce upon the ball when it comes loose.

The lone forward breaking through offers a special problem. If a defender is guarding the circle it will be wrong for the goalkeeper either to stay on his line or to go out so close to his colleague that their opponent beats them by the same manoeuvre simultaneously. He must move to a suitable position to tackle immediately should the defender be defeated. That defender must understand that his tackle should not be made so far outside the circle that the goalkeeper cannot use his feet, and that, if beaten, he must dash back to cover.

In meeting a forward in this situation, or on the circle edge without another defender available, the goalkeeper will try to force him onto his stick side. Chances of interception are increased and the forward may have to go wider, thus allowing a little more time in which another defender may be able to cover.

Facing the breakaway forward when no other defender can intervene is a severe test of a goalkeeper. Having decided to go out, he must go hard and fast, aiming to tackle his opponent by whatever is the most appropriate means just inside the circle. Good timing is necessary. If the goalkeeper uses his feet outside the circle it may well be construed as a deliberate offence and a penalty corner awarded.

Rapid acceleration over the last few yards may help him to catch the forward slightly off guard. He needs to be right up to his opponent, thereby depriving him of any worthwhile target (narrowing the angle).

It is usually poor 'keeping to be caught midway between forward and goal. My maxim is: If in doubt, go out. Intelligent anticipation of the build-up play helps to eliminate the doubt.

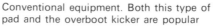

Conventional equipment. Both this type of pad and the overboot kicker are popular

Equipment

For fast movement after periods of inactivity, a goalkeeper needs to be warm. He must also be adequately protected, but not so weighed down that agility and mobility are significantly impaired.

Head

Face-masks have become fairly commonplace in the men's game. Whilst older goalkeepers will often scorn them, or find them too inconvenient, a case for their use may fairly be made. An umpire will forbid any which he considers might endanger players. The FIH recommend the moulded plastic type.
Mouth Protectors. See p. 13.
Cap. One with a suitable peak for rain or sun should be available. Long hair may similarly be controlled, though other measures may be necessary.

Body

Clothing needs to be comfortable as well as providing adequate warmth on cold days. Shirt, sweater and tracksuits all have their uses.

Abdominal protectors should be worn by male goalkeepers in all practices as well as matches. There are various types. Whichever is worn should not chafe in any way or interfere with movement.
Shorts or tracksuit bottoms again

depend on preference and weather.

Hands

Generally some sort of glove is worn. It should not interfere with the manipulation of the stick – a contra-indication to wicket-keeping gauntlets. Special gauntlets are made which offer protection well up the forearm. They are very expensive. They are, however, popular with men internationals.

Feet and Legs

All goalkeepers must wear pads. The conflict between mobility and protection, especially for men who have to stop very fierce shots, is considerable. For men, the Continental, open cane-work type are gaining in popularity. They are reinforced by padded rolls and, with square wings, present a flat front to the ball. Standard types with square wings are also available and much cheaper. Women will wear lighter ones, but whatever is worn should fit and have inside protection at the knee. Buckles fasten on the outside of the leg and the top strap should be just tight enough to stop the thigh portion from flapping about. Kickers are basically of the overboot or the cheaper flap type. Some goalkeepers place foam rubber padding under the flap types which, while offering a good deal less protection, are far lighter.

Boots need to be adequate for their task and strengthened toe caps are to be preferred. Good studs on the boots and on overboot-type kickers are essential.
Note: Detailed regulations covering certain items are contained in 'Personal Equipment' at the end of the Rule Book.

Practices

The following is a selection of useful practices.

1. Other Activities

These include soccer for kicking, squash and table tennis for reactions, and ballroom dancing which, given sufficient floor space, is excellent for footwork and balance.
Some may be adapted. 'Squash soccer' is squash played with the feet and a tennis ball. When serving from left use only that foot and only the right foot from the

right. Enjoyable and energetic. In normal hockey goalkeeping kit play soccer with a hockey ball in an area appropriate to the numbers available.

2. Stick Practices

Goalkeepers should always be included and should play out of goal from time to time. Relevant techniques can be practised at odd moments.

3. Kicking Practices

These are legion. Ensure both feet are used, especially the weaker. Examples:

a. Pass ball round a large revolving circle of players. Reverse the movement.

b. Target Man (see p. 65). This type of practice is easily adapted. Servers use any means for propelling ball. Goalkeeper must either return it accurately first time or control and return as fast as possible. Stick passing is allowable where appropriate but the emphasis is on kicking.

c. Kick a tennis ball against a wall and return. Try to keep it going without a break.

d. For direction. One server, plenty of balls and fielders. Ball is served gently. Before it arrives goalkeeper nominates the direction of his intended clearance. Later the server nominates but the service must be fair, e.g. do not serve outside his right foot if he is

required to clear 'square left'. Goalkeeper need not be in goal when he kicks and may be running out to clear.

4. Saving

These can often be combined with practices for the other players, but goalkeepers do need their own special sessions.

a. Server throws a quick succession of tennis balls from about the penalty stroke spot. The corners of the goal should be peppered and balls can be made to bounce awkwardly.
An agility exercise which speeds up reactions, given a fast tempo. Do *not* let goalkeeper strike at balls with his hand.
This can be made more severe by making the goalkeeper start from a sitting position to which he must return after every save. Make sure that he gets up from the ground. It should prove strenuous.

b. Goalkeeper stands on his line facing into goal. Servers stand around circle, or closer if

appropriate to goalkeeper's ability. One server shouts 'Coming' and delivers the ball in the way he chooses, including throwing or even using a cricket bat.
Goalkeeper spins round, saves and, where reasonable to do so without delaying the exercise, clears. Servers should not throw in set order. Essential that only ONE ball in use at a time. Tempo to be as rapid as circumstances permit.

5. Tackling

a. Goalkeeper on back edge of a grid. Attacker has to dribble round him in that grid. Series of attackers used, one after the other.

b. Attacker starts from twenty-five, goalkeeper from goal-line or other suitable point. Attacker has to score. May be conditioned so that it is compulsory to dribble past the goalkeeper.
After each of a series of attackers, goalkeeper runs *backwards* to starting point.

c. Combined with Clearing. Set up with goal 2 yds wide:

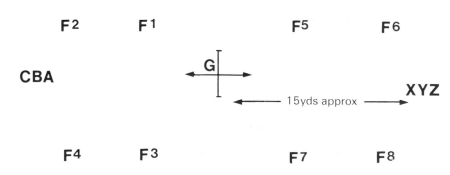

Goalkeeper meets first attacker, A. If he wins ball, he must try to clear accurately to a fielder suitably placed. Goalkeeper immediately runs back to deal with X and, after X, B etc. Fielders and attackers, both of whom may be varied in numbers, change round.

6. Combined Play

The defence should be trained to play together. Attack v. Defence may be used, but generally the attackers will need to be superior in numbers if goalkeeper is to be tested, e.g. 5 forwards+1 support player v. GK and 2 backs+a CB, depending on standards. Methods of awarding points to both sides may be devised and a couple of target men for the defenders' clearances introduced. They move along the half-way line.

Defenders are easily fitted into shooting practices and the goalkeeper will learn to work with them in corner and penalty corner practices.

Other exercises, such as two forwards approaching a single back supported by the goalkeeper, are also useful.

Opportunity should also be taken in appropriate practices to train defenders in covering the goalkeeper.

German goalkeeper in action. Note the Continental-type equipment

The Set-Pieces

Inevitably in hockey, because of the technical rules needed to cover the use of stick and ball, there will be more stoppages than in games in which various parts of the body control a much larger ball. The term 'set-pieces' embraces the methods of resuming play after such stoppages and after goals and accidents, besides the start of each half.

The bully apart, all have one important characteristic: they give undisputed possession to one team. In top level tournaments penalties per team may average over fifty per match. On such occasions it is even more culpable than in open play to squander that possession, especially as it usually occurs through lack of thought or care.

Edinburgh, 1975: Japan defending a penalty corner against Australia

General

In Attack

To make the most of these – possession set-pieces teams must:
- ■ Be alert – think
- ■ Move rapidly

These are inter-linked. Interruption of play easily breaks concentration. When the whistle blows players should not play on and certainly not hit the ball away. Instead they should simply look at the umpire for his directional signal and the nature of the award, if necessary. Childish behaviour, such as gestures of dissent, is worse than useless. It puts the player momentarily out of the game. Continuing concentration will enable players most quickly to think and decide where best to go – in defence as well as in attack. The aim of rapid movement is to have the team re-deployed by the greatest possible margin of time before their opponents. Slow reactions from players, arising from loss of concentration and sluggish thought, help opponents. Except where relief from pressure is the over-riding consideration, and at a penalty stroke, the re-deployment will be directed to maintaining possession for an almost immediate shot at goal – e.g. corners and penalty corners – or to building up play for a shot.

In Defence

Most of the foregoing applies. If the award is not to their liking, players with psychological deficiencies in self-discipline and composure are especially vulnerable to loss of concentration. The rapid thought and movement will be applied to containing the advantage given to the opponents.

At pushes-in and free hits there will most usually be a choice between marking an opponent, marking space, and covering. Accepting that on occasion defenders will be outnumbered, their first priority will be to deny the penetrating pass or the one to the most dangerously placed attacker. Next they will try to prevent any forward pass. Other passes do allow a little leeway for adjustment of marking or for extra defenders to take station.

Even at corners and penalty corners it can pay to get quickly into position. There may then be a short while to assess the intentions of the attackers and to become composed rather than being immediately engulfed in the urgency of play.

The Push-In

See Rule 17 (IV).

General

This, though not the most important set-piece, is taken first as clubs rarely give it any attention at all. The push-in replaced the roll-in for men in 1970 but is comparatively new to the women's game. Various experiments were tried before the push-in was introduced.

In Attack

Aim:

To mount an attack, generally with possession distant from the push-in. The vicinity of the push-in is often congested. Moving the ball away seeks to use the resultant space elsewhere. Occasionally a quickly-taken push-in in the Attack Area may lead to a shot from a nearby portion of the circle.

Support:

The key to success, as with many set-pieces. Without it no movement will work except by chance.

Players at a push-in fall into one of two groups:

Near – those in proximity to the push, say at 5–10 yds range. They are likely to receive the ball. They therefore have the responsibility of moving into position as fast as ever they can to avoid their markers. Even if they cannot escape they may still be able to open space.

Distant – the remainder, farther away. Though less likely than the near players to receive the push, they must be alert to the chance of the pusher-in passing to them. They are more likely to become involved in play subsequent to the actual push-in.

Central players, e.g. CF and CH/CM, often fail to look for gaps between the near players through which they may receive the push-in direct.

Taking the Push-In

1. Infringements

Any breach of the rules which surrenders possession is unforgivable, for the requirements are simple. Thoughtless crowding inside the 5 yds limit is also reprehensible. It causes delay and the possible loss of a good opportunity for starting an attack. Nevertheless, should opponents encroach, the team are entitled to the support of the umpire.

2. Technique

This is detailed on pp. 14–18. Faults sometimes arise through the stress of the moment. Practice is needed to push-in correctly and strongly, yet quickly. So, too, for disguised pushing. The reverse-push is in itself rather a weak stroke. When used it therefore needs to be played very firmly indeed.

3. The Pusher-In

This is one of three players:
- The one nearest the ball. This is put first to emphasise the great need for speed.
- WH/WB. From his own goal-line to within about 20 yds of the other.
- WF. For this last 20 yds in the Attack Area.

Far too often delay occurs whilst players debate who is to push. If the nearest player is not a wing player, the team will need to adjust dispositions accordingly. If the WH or WB takes the pushes deep in the Attack Area there is the double danger of the WF finding himself offside and the half being unable to intervene should the opponents win possession and counter-attack.

Tactics

Given an alert and co-operating team, the initiative is more likely to come from the other players than the pusher-in. It may still, however, be his and a *simple easily-remembered* code of signals may profitably be arranged beforehand. Three signals are sufficient. More than these, or complicated ones, will be forgotten in the heat of the game.
SPACE. Creating space is the fundamental facet of the operation. Players will try to:
- Reach a position where they can receive and pass freely.
- Open space into which they can

run to receive.
- Open space for a pass to someone else.

Inexperienced players may not relish running if the ball does not come to them. The value of such runs and of individual members working for the team as a whole will have to be explained.
The critical movements may be by one, two or more players. Some examples are as follows.

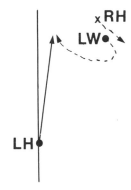

Here one man, LW, has stationed himself well in-field to persuade the marking RH to leave space for a pass up the line. In this particular case LW has started a dummy run to mislead RH, suddenly doubling back into space.
In the top diagram on p. 122 two players, LW and IL, have moved to take their markers with them on decoy runs, opening the way for a pass to either CF or CH, depending on the situation. If the markers do not conform, the decoy runners are free for a pass.

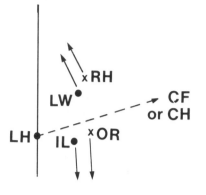

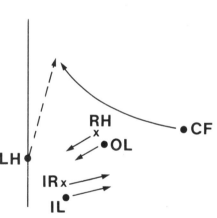

In the diagram directly above, three players are moving, two making decoy runs for the third, CF, to collect.

AREAS OF THE PITCH. These influence the type of pass which may be used.

Defence Area. The main criterion is security. No push-in should be used which, if missed or fumbled, would put the circle in jeopardy.

Basically, therefore, the ball should be sent *forwards*, within about a 45° arc, preferably up the line. Only on rare occasions should the short diagonal pass to the back be tried, and the player *must be absolutely clear* of any attacker. Normally he will be marked by or within reach of the opposing WF.

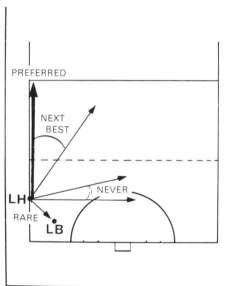

Pushes-in in the Defence Area

Build-up Area. This offers greater scope, in fact an arc of 180°. Any of the suggested moves may be made. In developing the attack the chances are highest in this Area via the other flank. It often happens that the push-in reaches CH, who is well placed to switch the point of attack.

Attack Area. Because marking is likely to be extra tight and because of the proximity of the goal-line, considerations affecting the creation and use of space have special point. The general tactical maxims of getting in behind the defence and of offering defenders the greatest chances of making mistakes also apply strongly. Defenders' errors may well produce free hits or corners. Pressure will encourage such errors.

A typical example arises on the right (see diagram **a**). X may well have difficulty near his left foot and edge the ball behind for a corner. He may also cause obstruction, provided that IR makes *a genuine attempt* to play the ball.

On the other side, possible pushes by LW from two specimen positions are shown. Push (a) attempts to get behind the defence and a space-making decoy run, as by IL to move RB to the wing, may be needed. Pushes (b) are for others to run on to and shoot. From position 1 or 2 OL may push diagonally back to LH.

Developing Attacks. The use of CH in switching play has already been mentioned. Obviously it could just as well be another player, as in diagram **b**. Space must be quite open for this pass. Frequently CF can help by moving up-field, taking CH with him.

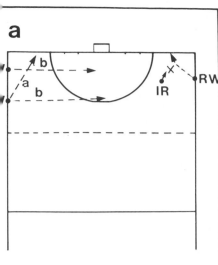

a

hes-in in the Attack Area
s edged the ball behind

development from a push-in

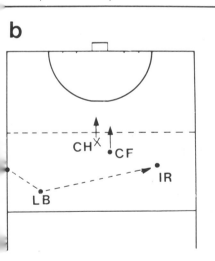

b

he pusher-in himself may play an
portant role. He is often
vailable for a return pass from a
ear team-mate as no one usually

specifically marks him. He can
distribute by a hit, or, in suitable
circumstances, a scoop over the
marking half to his wing.

Conclusion

Maintaining concentration will
assist speed of thought, decision
and movement to produce
optimum support to create usable
space. Players need to move and,
excluding possibly those most
distant, not to assume static
positions unless part of a plan,
e.g. for the pass 'through' them.
All legal ruses and deceptions
should be employed. These may
include a switch of the player
pushing-in. The one apparently
due to take it darts off suddenly,
leaving it to another. This one
must, however, wait until his
colleague is 5 yds away before
pushing.
Although the initiative will usually
be from the other players, the final
decision is with the pusher-in. To
make this correctly he must scan
the whole area. In doing so he
may be able to mislead opponents
by how and where he looks. He
may also add to the deception by
standing back from the ball until
the last moment.

In Defence

Aim:
To regain possession by
interception or by winning the ball
from an opponent.

Tasks:
To some extent the
opponents govern the teams'
dispositions. Nevertheless the
players still form the same two
broad groups:
Near—to deny continued
possession and to deny space for
longer passes.
Distant—to cover gaps in the
ring, to mark dangerous opponents
such as CF and CH and to guard
the approach to the circle.

Marking and Cover:

Possible deployments of both
sides where a speedy push-in
could not be taken are shown
below.

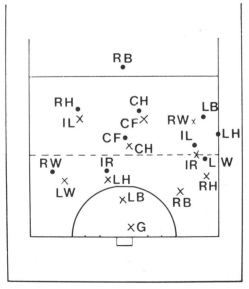

Belgium pushing-in against Pakistan at Montreal. Note: (a) No. 3 is unmarked; (b) The judges' table—only the sticks in front of it, already checked by them, will be permitted as replacements; (c) Management bench with substitutes; (d) Score-board

All the attackers, except the pusher-in, are marked man for man. RB guards direct access to the circle with LB giving deep cover. X IL could be back on the opposing IR. This would free X LH for extra deep cover, or, if LW had not returned, for marking RW. All that has been said about maintaining concentration and speed in attack applies to defence. Defenders must be as fast as attackers. Each defender has to pick up 'his' attacker. Alternatively, the near defenders use a zonal system to ring the area round the push taking whichever opponent enters their zone. Markers must be aware of attackers trying to reach blind side positions.

Free Hits

Rule 14, governing free hits, contains the only differences between the rules for men and women. They are:

a) Strokes

Whereas men may only hit or push along the ground, women may use any legitimate stroke, though when propelled into the circle the ball must not rise above knee height.

b) Position

Mostly the hit is taken on the same spot as the infringement. The exceptions are:

Men. If the hit has been awarded within 16 yds of their goal line, it may be taken from any spot within that distance on a line drawn through the point of the infringement from the goal line and parallel to the side line.

Women. When the offence is within the defenders' circle, they may take the hit from anywhere inside it.

Avoid losing possession needlessl by breaking the Rule.

Much of what has been said unde The Push-In (above) applies to the free hit, though because of the more fluid situation of the fre hit, the division of team-mates into rear and distant is less relevan Additionally, the following are stressed.

In Attack

Aim:

Depending on the tactical contex to sustain an attack, mount an attack or relieve pressure.

Support:

Especially in maintaining the impetus of an attack, support mus be rapid. So often a player is blamed for a bad free hit when n one gave him any support. In all but rare instances, at least one player must give close support to the hitter. Often a player runs onto the pass, coming from behin

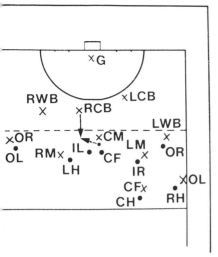

Developing the hit

CB has received the hit in last diagram. Possibilities include those illustrated.

RCB passes to RWB, who by moving ightly inwards facilitates his own upfield ass. CM runs at IL to hold his attention. R's run takes OL away to the wing before e cuts back inside. RM's run also idens space. RWB must allow for the dvancing LB (off diagram) coming up to ock the threatened break through

Free hit

Ball with CM. All his own men in front of him are marked, but RCB can move on to pass

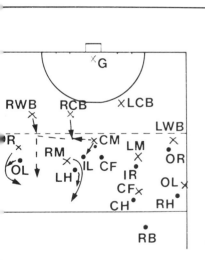

Tactics

So much depends on the speed with which the players and the ball get into position.

As with passing generally, the hitter should be looking first for the penetrating or at least the forward pass. Especially where delay in taking the hit has been unavoidable, this will not always be feasible. For instance, see the diagrams on the left. Such situations again stress the value of close support, especially from a deeper player moving forwards. Every legitimate method to effect surprise should be exploited. For example, a player other than the one ostensibly preparing to take the hit actually does so. An example:

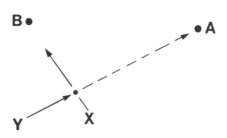

X, standing near the ball, indicates —though not so obviously as to invite suspicion—his intention of passing to B. He steps forward but runs on past the ball, leaving Y to move quickly onto it and pass to A. Or X may be able to find space for Y to pass to him. Various other ideas can be used.

AREAS OF THE PITCH
Defence Area

Special problems often arise, particularly towards the side line, in turning the hit to appreciable advantage. The principle of security will rule out a number of somewhat speculative passes justifiable in other Areas. Additionally, as when a powerful opposing attack has broken down, adequate support for the hitter may be numerically deficient.

For hits within the circle women should use their option to the full. Quickly throwing the ball from the point of the offence, where congestion is likely, across the circle, may offer far greater scope, notably when advanced players have been quick enough to foresee and react.

Usually such hits are taken on the circle edge. Players should, however, be alert for opportunities profitably to take them from deeper positions. These are most likely to arise when, again, advanced players have retreated in anticipation. See top left diagram on p. 126.

This switching may also be very helpful when a player is able to use a long aerial pass.

As a general precept the wing on the flank concerned should always be prepared to go *well* back for

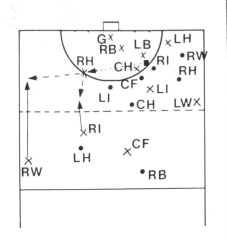

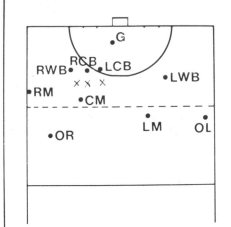

Women's free hit in the circle
■ =Position of offence.
LB promptly throws ball to RH. In
anticipation, both RW and RI have raced
back to receive possible hit from RH

all such hits, at 16-yds hit outs and
similar free hits. This means at
least level with, and *preferably
slightly behind square* of, the
hitter. There are two reasons. First,
the wing is more likely to shake off
marking. Secondly, he is more
likely — because it is easier for the
hitter — to receive the ball in front of
him. Many 16-yds hits are directed
badly so that the wing has to try
to gather the ball from behind.
Usually it goes needlessly into
touch.
Nevertheless, a deliberate hit into
touch, as long a one as is possible,
should not be despised when
nothing better exists.
Opponents will be keen to ring
the hit (see p. 127) to try to
maintain pressure. A popular
counter is shown above right.
If this hit were in the middle and
this method used, probably CM,

16-yards hit — countering the ring
The three Xs cannot stop the ball going to
RWB or LCB or forward.
  Specimen supporting positions for
developing the movement are also
shown.
  Note G poised for emergencies

flanked by the two CBs, would
take it.
Another method is to insert a
player into the arc.

Build-up Area
Much of what has been written
above and much of what follows
under Attack Area applies with
necessary adaptation. When a
good forward pass is not available
one played wide to a wing may
lead indirectly to a strike at goal
because of the need for the
opponents to re-position.

Attack Area
The value of the fast free hit is
greatest when an attack has been
interrupted by an unintentional
offence near the opponents' circle
and sufficient players are

available to offer a good chance
of reaching the circle to shoot.
The position may be much more
static and the whole operation
much more deliberate. Given the
chance, which may well be
unavoidable, defenders will flock
back to mark dangerous attackers
and to deny them time and space.
Very few club teams lay any plan
to combat a favourably placed

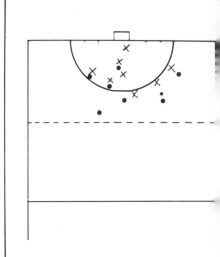

Typical situation at a free hit in inside
position — attackers crowded into middle
half of pitch

defence. This sort of picture
occurs regularly. The defence do
not have to deny space; the
attackers are voluntarily
surrendering it. Nor has the man

taking the hit any *useful* close support, whereas the operational triangles of the defence are closely linked.

Thoughtful movement can greatly increase the attacking possibilities. One example is:

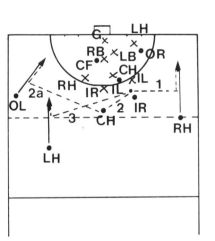

A much improved attacking deployment

The aim is to turn a flank, using available space.

OR has entered the circle apparently crowding in still more, but really to open wing space. CH has come well behind square to improve his own chances of receiving a pass (Pass 2), with the possibility of switching to the left wing (Pass 2a). OL has withdrawn well away from the circle, ostensibly uninterested in the proceedings. If OL has been

tracked down by the opposing OR, LH comes out of his covering position – which he can safely do – at speed to take Pass 3. RH is in fairly close support. Warned by his OR's position, he is ready to burst on to Pass 1 for a right hook.

In Defence

Members of the defending team have three possible tasks:

Ringing the Hit

This reduces the angles, especially the forward ones, to the hitter. Usually about three players move into an arc between the hitter and their goal. The distance will

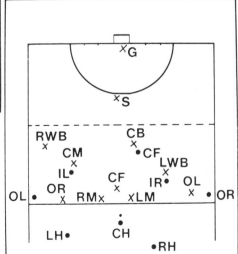

Ringing the hit
Central position, three men in the ring. All defenders goalside, two (RWB and S) in covering roles

depend on the likely power of the hitter and individual stopping ability – improved by having the blade grounded. Probably distances are about 10 yds for men and less for women. Women, by standing close to the hitter, may prevent her using a high scoop because of its being dangerous.

Marking

Backs, halves and midfields pick up their own opponents as necessary. Inside forwards are also involved and, at critical stages, or when the hit is well upfield, the other forwards too.

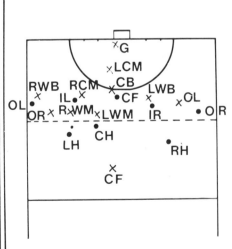

Defending free hit near twenty-five
Based on a position from play in a tournament final, near the end with Xs winning. They adopted a blanket defence with only CF uncommitted. (They were playing 3–4–3)

In the last diagram on p. 127, every man in advance of the hitter, LH, is closely marked, except OR, whom X OL can easily reach as any pass to him arrives. The ring is only X OR and RWM.

Cover

This is most often the duty of the backs/centre-backs, though they may be needed in man-marking roles. In the above diagram only LCM was covering (CB stayed with CF). Women in deep positions may need to be alive to the use of the aerial pass.
As situations vary so widely, depending on the positions of both teams and of the ball, hard and fast rules cannot be laid down to cater for every eventuality. In essence the fundamental requirements of the team are:

● Speed. Aim to redeploy faster than the opponents.
● Ability to recognise the most dangerous threat — contain this first.
● Penetration — block forward passes.

Speed of thought — as well as of action — is necessary to evaluate these sometimes conflicting demands rapidly. Then, the greater the flexibility and understanding of the team the greater their effectiveness in nullifying their opponents' advantage.

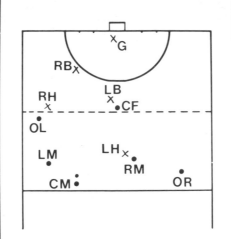

Containing dangerous threats
Outnumbered Xs must do the best they can. The three most dangerous men have been picked up, LH deliberately leaving OR. RB covers

Penalty Corners

Rule 15 describes the procedure for taking penalty corners. Rules 10 (Penalties, 2), 12 (Penalties, 3), 14 (Penalties, 1), 17 I, II (Penalties) and III lay down when they shall be awarded. The commonest cases are for unintentional infringements within the circle by a defender not preventing a probable goal.
In men's hockey especially many matches are won on penalty corners. At top level only about 1·5 seconds are needed for the ball to be put in, be stopped and hit the goal-board.

In Attack

Aim: Quite simply to score!

This may be with the shot itself or in follow-up play.
Much practice is required. The success of outstanding penalty corner strikers has not come by chance. A few minutes' practice before a game is woefully inadequate. In men's hockey the penalty corner 'team' is often considered to consist of three people: one to propel the ball off the goal line, another to hand-stop it and the third to shoot. A coverer of the stopper should be included. Their duties follow below. Every side should contain trained, competent deputies.
In women's hockey hand stopping is used far more rarely.

Men's Standard Drill

(i.e. hit or push-in, hand-stop and shot)

FOR THE SHOT

1. Hitter-In/Pusher-In

Most conveniently the WF. He must propel the ball flat, hard and accurately, otherwise he immediately jeopardises the whole operation. The target is the stopper's hand. Practise hitting drink cans or end-on bricks at 16 yds range. Whether you use hit or push depends largely on personal choice and ground conditions. The push reduces the warning given to defenders but its user must be capable of generating sufficient pace and of not lifting the ball. Warning with the hit can

Hand-stopping

also be reduced by starting with stick raised and weight back. Usually the hit or push is made from the attacker's left side of the goal because of factors affecting the stopper and shooter.

2. Stopper

From a crouched position he offers his left hand as the target. As the hit-in is made, he runs several steps into the circle. Since the late sixties, this position for stopping the ball has gained in popularity. The stopper needs to crouch low with the back of the ends of his fingers on the ground and wrist loose and forward. This reduces the possibility of a rebound – a foul. His hand and wrist can give a little as he momentarily grasps the ball to stop it. When the hand is used the ball must be stopped absolutely dead and on the ground.

If the ball is bumping on an indifferent surface the only safe answer is to *forget the hand-stop*. The main alternatives are to use a variation (see below) with a stick-stop being made at some point or other before the actual shot, or for the shooter to stick-stop the ball himself. Occasionally someone may do a stick-stop for him.

In stopping with the stick some latitude is afforded.

Once he has stopped the ball it is the stopper's duty to move rapidly out of the shooter's way.

3. Shooter

Modern thinking holds that the shot should be made from a spot about opposite the centre of the goal. This offers the best possible target. Running into the shot adds power.

Above all else, the shot must be on target. To be off-target is unpardonable. If the shot is on target but does not go into goal, there may well be the chance of scoring from a rebound or from a deflection. The stop will not always be exactly to the shooter's liking. He should re-position if possible, but rather than swing wildly, he must go for accuracy, even if power is lost. Sometimes a flick may be preferable.

Finally, when necessary, the shooter must be proficient at stopping the ball for himself.

4. Coverer

He stations himself on the line of the hit-in behind the stopper to collect any ball not stopped. He can then either enter the circle – if not already in – and shoot, or pass to someone else, he and the receiver remembering that the ball must be stopped somewhere before one of them shoots.

An England penalty corner against Wales. A vindication of those preferring to use both backs to defend the goal!

THE ASSAULT WAVE (sometimes called the 'second phase')

Five players are directly concerned. Their intention is to form an arc round the goalkeeper to snap up rebounds. Usually they will close in to 2–3 yds. Being closer gives little chance of picking up the line of the rebound.

Those concerned are:

- move on-side as fast as possible and who therefore runs on an arc.
- in front of the goalkeeper.
- One player starting from between the hitter-in and stopper.

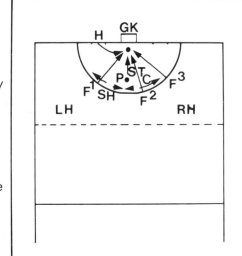

Assault wave (second phase positions)

P : Point of stop and shot
H : Hitter-in
SH : Shooter
ST : Stopper
F : Other forwards
C : Coverer
F³ should be especially alive to the chance of deflecting in any shot going wide

- Two players running in from the stopper's right, one of whom must be well round the circle. If the ball is not saved by the goalkeeper these players will adjust accordingly. The striker polices the head of the circle for long rebounds or attempted clearances. The coverer assists him. Wing halves try to return flank clearances into the circle.

A shot variation which should be used more. A Japanese about to flick in the Edinburgh Tournament, 1975

The remaining two out-players deploy to guard against breakouts, probably near the half-way line, though one may give deep cover.

Lastly, the goalkeeper should come well off his line to note the general defensive plan of the opponents, especially to discern any weaknesses. He should also note any shortcomings amongst his own men.

Variations

These are legion. They are used either to mislead the opposition or, when the standard is failing, to produce better results.

Only a few specimens are given. Many others can be devised by teams to suit themselves. It is mistaken policy to have a wide

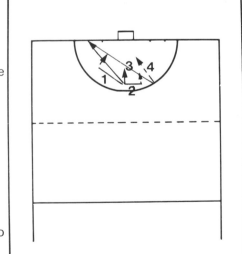

Variations from the left

1 Especially to exploit any suitable space left to GK's right rear. Either hitter-in comes back to shoot or LH runs onto the shot
2 Stopped and pushed across for first-time shot
3 After the stop, ball rolled gently forward, short of GK, for first-time shot. Possibility when stop is unfavourable for shooter's normal hit
4 Hit-in direct to man in IR position

repertoire – in a match some players are bound to forget some of them. Any variation needs practice. Each player must know his role in every one. Furthermore, he must realise which is to be used at a given moment. *Simple* signals will help.

Some players prefer to shoot from the right side of the circle with the natural swing of the stick.

Complications arise from the position of the hand-stopper.

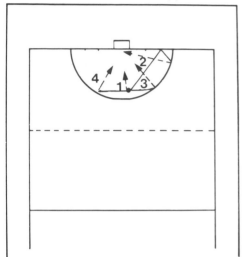

Variations from the right
1 Standard drill transposed from left
2 Using man up close to hitter-in. He may shoot if GK is badly placed, dribble in or pass in various directions
3 For RH – or a very good shot – running up from well away
4 Stopped and pushed across for first-time shot. Stopper can stop with left hand and, without rising, push one-handed with right

In Defence

Aim :—To prevent a goal, either directly or indirectly, in follow-up play.
    —As a subsidiary to that, and bearing in mind that security is the first priority, to launch a counter-attack whenever possible.

For the first part of the aim the six players behind the goal-line must work to an organised plan. For the second they need the help of the five over the half-way line.

Methods

Many have been used over the years and it is unlikely that the last word has been said on the subject. All, however, stressed three points concerning the goalkeeper. He needed to:
■ Advance to narrow the angle
■ Have a clear sight of the ball for the actual shot, and during any follow-up play
■ Be poised to save and not moving when the shot came.
He is the most important player in this action. He should be consulted before a plan is finally adopted and during the set-piece itself his calls and instructions must be instantly obeyed.
To counter the two phases of the attacker's plan, whatever defensive method is used can logically also be divided into two:
1. STOPPING THE SHOT
There are two possibilities:
Preventing the Shot
One particularly fast player, often a forward, goes hard and resolutely for the ball on the head of the circle. If it is a forward, he and the player with whom he has changed places should retain their new positions until a suitable opportunity occurs for them to switch back.

This fast defender will start from one of two positions. If he has decided to go in on his stick side, it will most probably be from the goal on the goalkeeper's left. He will admittedly be running up the cone of fire but he will not unsight the goalkeeper unless it is just as he tackles. He may choose, or the goalkeeper may ask him to do so, to start from close to but just outside the right post. This is less favourable for him, but is his starting point if at the outset he decides for a reverse-stick tackle. Some clubs use a second player as a definite follow-up wave slightly behind and outside the first to collect any ball pushed passed him or across to the (defenders') right.
Saving the Shot
Assuming the first man out is unsuccessful in preventing the shot coming in, the following applies :
● Goalkeeper. He has to reduce the size of the goal by advancing, yet still give himself time in which to react effectively to the shot. Up to about 5 yds is generally considered the best distance but with personal variation.
Most goalkeepers will start from the centre of their goal, running out in line with the anticipated stopping point. If they go quickly they will have time to adjust should the ball be transferred left or right and still be stationary,

poised to receive the shot.

● Backs. The standard men's drill is to use both backs to protect the dangerous area of the goal just inside the posts. First, they must come forward off the line, for if they remain behind it and are struck on the shins it is a goal. Secondly, they must not allow any shot to pass between them and the post.

They therefore advance a couple of paces towards the shooter with their outside leg virtually in line with the post. By doing this they will also:

—Narrow the angle, together reducing the target by about 25 per cent.

—Give themselves some chance of retrieving a partly stopped ball.

—Be better placed to help the goalkeeper with rebounds.

Club sides may be able to free one back from this close defence task. If only one is retained it will be the back farther from the shot, or, if the shot is taken centrally, generally the LB to help on the goalkeeper's non-stick side.

2. FOLLOW-UP PLAY

Far more shots are saved, or miss the target, than go into goal. Having a sound plan to effect clearances is of prime importance. Defenders are therefore deployed

to cover all areas as far as possible. These areas are most readily described by the conception of a cross with the handle offset along the circle from the point of the shot to the centre of the goal. The arms are at right-angles through the position of the goalkeeper. Each defender is responsible for the areas shown. The axis of the cross would move round from the stopping point to the shooting point should the ball be switched, and necessary adjustments in players' positioning made.

The following points should be noted:—

■ Cone of Fire. Must be kept free to allow the goalkeeper and

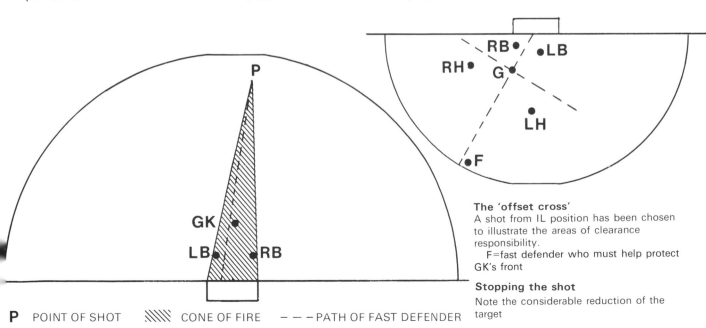

The 'offset cross'
A shot from IL position has been chosen to illustrate the areas of clearance responsibility.

F=fast defender who must help protect GK's front

Stopping the shot
Note the considerable reduction of the target

P POINT OF SHOT \\\\\\\ CONE OF FIRE – – – PATH OF FAST DEFENDER

backs uninterrupted sight of the ball.

■ Wing Halves, or those who may have taken over these roles for the time being, will be aiming for positions about 5 yds and 45° from the goalkeeper. As they advance, they must be prepared to challenge should the ball be switched to someone in their sector.

■ Goalkeeper. He must be very agile in moving rapidly to clear anything he can reach himself.

■ Fast Defender. He must not leave the circle until the danger is over, but come back to help the goalkeeper.

■ Backs. The one nearer the hitter-in should specially watch this player. When the variation of switching the ball to him is used, he has an excellent scoring chance if unchallenged.

■ Divided Responsibility. When the rebound is on the dividing line of players' responsibilities, the nearer one should take it. This notably applies when it is on his forehand. Indeed, it may well pay for the forehand player to take the ball even if appreciably farther away than the player with it on his reverse. Clear calling should avoid confusion.

Recommended starting positions and movements are as in the diagram above right.

Defenders' starting positions and movements for a central shot hit in from attackers' left.

F¹ and F² show alternative positions for fast defender

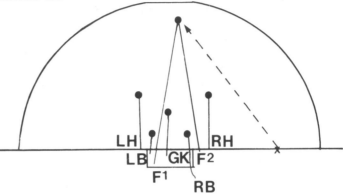

VARIATIONS

When these are used, defenders should still have three basic aims:

● To challenge the shooter
● To guard the goal
● To clear rebounds.

For instance, suppose the stop and shot are made farther round the circle, say the attacker's inside-left position. The fast man out could start opposite, outside the defenders' right post. A player could then go from the goalkeeper's left with the responsibility of protecting his front and of challenging any switch across goal.

Again, some goalkeepers may feel able to allow the back nearer to the shot to leave his post and advance several yards. The back would be able to intervene quicker in follow-up play, but would have to be careful not to impede the goalkeeper's movements.

THE COUNTER-ATTACK

The players beyond the half-way line have important functions, though regrettably in club games these five seem lamentably unaware of what is required. First they must race back to assist their team-mates. The longer the ball is in the circle the greater their chance of intervention. The wings and insides dash back as fast as they can to within their own twenty-five at least, adjusting en route, to receive any clearance. They may also be able to tackle attackers outside the circle trying to retrieve loose balls.

The CF will not retire so far. He will remain in the Build-Up Area, veering towards the location of the ball. His object is to take a pass in space. If he does he will need rapid support.

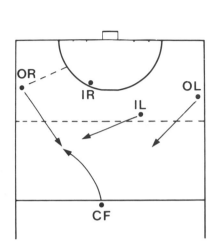

Specimen counter-attack
Follow-up play in the circle has allowed defending forwards to come well back, OR receiving the eventual clearance. He has passed to CF who has come ball side of the field. IL and OL have set off to support CF

Women

Although much of what has been said about male methods may be adapted, physical differences between the sexes are largely responsible for important changes, especially at club level.
Women do not generate the same speed and power, nor is the hand stop generally used.

IN ATTACK

Because the shot itself is far less deadly, more reliance is placed on variation. Again, however, a wide repertoire does not help. The standard shot is taken farther round the circle towards the left inner position. As man-to-man marking automatically means space is available, this may be exploited on the lines suggested below.

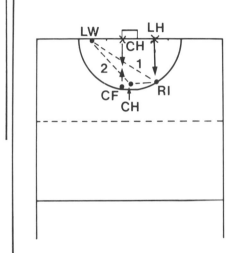

Space behind CF
CF runs forward to draw her marker so that LW can reach CH, moving up to shoot from CF's usual position, either via RI (1) or direct (2). In (1), RI, as a further variation, could shoot, given a reasonable opportunity

Wider round the circle a WH could come in to receive a pass from the stopper and shoot, with a reasonable chance of being unmarked. See above right.

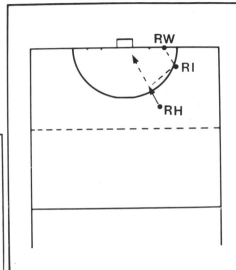

If a WH is so used, other members of the team must be particularly alive to the need for cover on her side should the move break down. A variation, for when the opponents were countering the use of RH, would be for LW not to run in on the goalkeeper for rebounds but to stay for a pass from RI.

Note, both sexes: Although positions have been allocated in these illustrations, the names refer to the players in them at that time. It is worth having the best available players to undertake the vital roles of hitter-in and shooter – plus hand-stopper if employed – regardless of their positions.

135

IN DEFENCE

With less immediate threat to the goal at least one and usually both backs are released from its close defence. This facilitates a basically man-to-man defensive system which provides greater cover against variations. With players lining up opposite the sticks — for that is where they will receive the ball — of their individual opponents, a typical method is shown below.

A Welsh defensive line-up

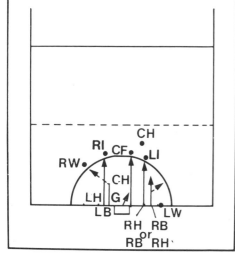

Whoever is faster, RB or RH, goes out at full speed to tackle LI, the other following to her side ready both to defeat any dodge by LI past her partner and to intercept any attempted pass to LW.
CH may start from inside or just outside the right post, making for CF, the first two going from her right.

To deal with RI, LH goes from outside the left post. From G's left LB advances to guard against the ball being played through the first wave or the opponent dodging through on her side. She also needs to watch RW.
With both backs in front of G it is more difficult for attackers, especially LW, to keep onside. G positions herself much as her male counterpart. A slower goalkeeper unable to 'explode' out of goal may try to compensate by moving farther than normal towards the shooter. This most probably will mean she is still moving forward as the shot is fired. She will thus not be able to adjust sideways as she would if she were stationary and poised.

With so many players going out between her and the shot, she is much more likely to be unsighted than in the men's standard defence. Those involved must do all they can to reduce this interference to the minimum.

Corners

General

Unlike the penalty corner (short corner), a corner ('long' corner) is awarded only in one set of circumstances. As Rule 17, II puts it, that is when the ball is 'sent unintentionally over the goal-line by or off one of the defending team who is within his own 25

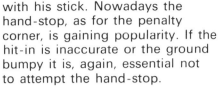

West Germany adopting a more masculine defensive formation against England. What is wrong with the positions of the backs?

yards area ... unless a goal has been scored'. The corner is governed by this Rule and Rule 15 and is taken from the side of the goal where the ball went out at a spot on the goal- or side-line within 5 yds of the corner flag. Most of the considerations affecting the penalty corner apply, sometimes with adaptation, to the corner.

In Attack

Hit-In

The push is usually confined to playing the ball short (see diagram, variations 3 (a) and (b)). The short pass is used more at corners than penalty corners. It is generally accepted that if the hit

is made from the goal-line, as against the side-line, it approaches the striker at a more favourable shooting angle.

The Stop

Previously, the shooter most frequently stopped the ball himself

with his stick. Nowadays the hand-stop, as for the penalty corner, is gaining popularity. If the hit-in is inaccurate or the ground bumpy it is, again, essential not to attempt the hand-stop.

The Shot

The standard drill merits most attention and practice.

Variations

See the diagram below, which shows some of the many possibilities:

1. Standard.
2. Straight across goal for indirect effect of keeping opponents guessing in future.
3. The receiver of this short pass has many options. He can centre across goal or angled beyond the far post, or pass to any open player. 3a indicates these. In 3b he takes the ball

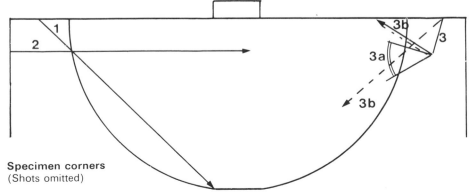

Specimen corners
(Shots omitted)

137

towards the goal-line — he may also dribble into the circle before acting as in 3a. He must assess the situation, but the hitter-in will have moved into the inside position in case of receiving a pass back.

Assault Wave

A nicer sense of timing may be called for than in penalty corners, because of the slightly longer period involved. The momentary pause will be of added value when the angle of the shot is switched or a manoeuvre based on variation 3 is used. If possible, adjustments should be made to collect rebounds on the forehand.

In Defence

Some opponents may prefer to strike from farther round the circle towards the hitter-in. It may then be better for the fast defender to start out of goal opposite the shooter. Also, given the probability of a short pass it may pay to have a wide defender able to challenge quickly and to bar they entry to the circle. The normal first man out may need to adjust his run or positioning to help.

The Penalty Stroke

Rule 16 gives details of this set-piece, which is most often awarded for a deliberate breach of the rules in the circle by a defender or for an unintentional one preventing a probable goal. In men's hockey it has grown in importance because of its widespread use to settle drawn competitive matches.

Prior to 1975, men played the stroke at 8 yds from goal. That year they came into line with the women to take it from 7.

In Attack

Given good technique, every penalty stroke should produce a goal. Failure, even allowing for the occasional brilliant save, is due to poor technique — usually arising from lack of practice. The most stupid way to throw away this excellent scoring chance is to break Rule 16. Common faults include not waiting for the umpire's signal before taking it, excessive delay after his whistle, and taking more than the stipulated one pace. The hit, for reasons of safety, is not allowed. Any other stroke is permitted and the ball may be raised to any height. The flick is the most popular. The essentials are power and accuracy; the powerful, accurate flick goes straight into goal. Power may beat the goalkeeper for pace or it may carry the ball on into goal even if he manages just to touch it. Any fair deception allowed by the Rule will enhance the possibility of success. It may be achieved by the eyes, the stance at the ball, and, most importantly, by body movement in making the stroke. Whilst some authorities recommend the attacker to stand at the ball and to play it without taking a pace into it, the single pace allowed is more often taken. With the player standing at the ball with stick in contact, the goalkeeper receives no indication of line of flight, there are fewer movements and therefore less scope for error. The use of the trunk and hips can markedly aid deception.

The preferred targets are the corners of the goal. Against a goalkeeper holding his stick in one hand, the ideal target is the top corner of the hand holding the stick. In trying to save, the goalkeeper might well give 'sticks'. If this prevented the ball going in, a penalty goal would be awarded. If the lower corners are selected the ball should be aimed at a height between the goalkeeper's ankle and knee. Practice is essential. For ordinary games, teams should ensure they have two specialists available. For critical games in men's tournaments, five are required.

India taking a penalty stroke against the eventual silver medallists, Australia, at Montreal

In Defence

The goalkeeper should approach his task with calm determination, accepting it as a challenge he may well win.

He may try to outwit his opponent by seeming unintentionally to be standing nearer one post than the other, so encouraging a shot at the bigger gap, for which he is really fully prepared.

He should stand with his heels on the line. This satisfies the Rule but allows him some chance of retrieving an only partially stopped ball. Once the umpire has blown for the stroke to be taken, both feet must be absolutely still. If he moves them, the shot which does not go in may be retaken or even a penalty goal awarded.

The stick should be held at about waist-height in both hands. For a high shot the appropriate hand can then be used without dropping the stick. It is easier to move the stick down than to lift it from the ground.

Many penalty goals are awarded for the illegal use of the hand (see p. 43). It is difficult to prevent striking at the ball when it occurs automatically, but any goalkeeper exhibiting this tendency in open play should do all he can to eliminate it. Apart from other exercises to improve reflexes, goalkeepers should miss no opportunity to practise defending strokes against the best exponents available.

Bibliography

The following books are recommended for further reading.

Women

AEWHA. Publications, *Guide Lines for Coaching Hockey.*

AEWHA. Publications, *Women's Hockey* in the National Westminster Bank Sport Coaching Series (Training & Education Associates Ltd., 41 Paradise Walk, London SW3 4JW, 1973).

Marjorie Cadel, *Coaching Hockey – an ABC* (Marjorie Pollard Publications, 1972).

Rachael Heyhoe, *Just for Kicks: Handbook for Hockey Goalkeepers* (JFK, The Hockey Field, Whitemilnes, Kencot, Lechlade, Glos., 1967).

Men

Hockey Association, *Hockey Coaching, Revised Edition, 1975* (Hodder & Stoughton). The official Manual of the HA. An entirely rewritten edition is planned for 1978.

Hockey Association, *Men's Hockey* in the National Westminster Bank Sport Coaching Series (Training & Education Associates Ltd., 41 Paradise Walk, London SW3 4JW, 1974).

Trevor Clarke, *Hockey: Teaching and Playing* (Lepus Books, 1976).

Horst Wein, *The Science of Hockey* (Pelham Books, 1973).

Note

1. Difficulties are sometimes encountered in local bookshops. Most of these books are, however, available from Marjorie Pollard Publications, Whitemilnes, Kencot, Lechlade, Glos. GL7 3QT.
2. Readers are advised to check latest prices when ordering.